PETER GABRIEL

The Reverb series looks at the connections between music, artists and performers, musical cultures and places. It explores how our cultural and historical understanding of times and places may help us to appreciate a wide variety of music, and vice versa.

reverb-series.co.uk
Series editor: John Scanlan

Already published

The Beatles in Hamburg
Ian Inglis

Brazilian Jive: From Samba to Bossa and Rap
David Treece

Easy Riders, Rolling Stones: On the Road in America, from Delta Blues to '70s Rock
John Scanlan

Gypsy Music: The Balkans and Beyond
Alan Ashton-Smith

Heroes: David Bowie and Berlin
Tobias Rüther

Jimi Hendrix: Soundscapes
Marie-Paule Macdonald

Neil Young: American Traveller
Martin Halliwell

Nick Drake: Dreaming England
Nathan Wiseman-Trowse

Peter Gabriel: Global Citizen
Paul Hegarty

Remixology: Tracing the Dub Diaspora
Paul Sullivan

Sting: From Northern Skies to Fields of Gold
Paul Carr

Tango: Sex and Rhythm of the City
Mike Gonzalez and Marianella Yanes

Van Halen: Exuberant California, Zen Rock'n'roll
John Scanlan

PETER GABRIEL

GLOBAL CITIZEN

PAUL HEGARTY

REAKTION BOOKS

Published by Reaktion Books Ltd
Unit 32, Waterside
44–48 Wharf Road
London N1 7UX, UK
www.reaktionbooks.co.uk

First published 2018

Printed and Bound in Great Britain by Bell & Bain, Glasgow

A catalogue record for this book is available from the British Library

ISBN 978 1 78023 976 7

CONTENTS

PREFACE: GENETICS

Everyone likes a beginning. We all like to know where someone starts, and we think it will help us pin them down for good. Both individuals and peoples regard the place of their birth as important, and imagine that everything else accrues to this essential being, a gathering of experiences of place around a fixed core, the rock in the snowball. These common-sense conceptions of place, of location, do not do justice to how Peter Gabriel locates himself in space, in time, in the world. If we were just to look at his beginnings, we would see a series of locations in prosperous southern England, set in the period just after the Second World War. Gabriel was born on 13 February 1950, and he has nearly always been resident in southern England, moving westward over time. In his case, we might want to hear those beginnings in the Anglican and Anglo phenomenon of progressive rock, exemplified in the band Genesis, of whom Gabriel was a founder member, vocalist and principal lyricist, and with whom he recorded six studio albums, leaving in 1975. But how much can we regard these stories as determining? In the case of Peter Gabriel, maybe we cannot get very far without regarding the ideas of place and locatedness as being in flux.

In fact, that particular origin story is too simple, and almost misleading in its presumptions about the musician and about the genre of music he began with. We do not need to accept such a narrative, as the roots attributed to progressive rock, often by its enemies, and mostly in hindsight, are way too simplistic. It is plain to any deeper consideration that the England of the 1960s from which one strain of progressive rock emerged was a much more complex and less culturally predictable place than it had seemed to be in the past. Similarly, progressive rock was heavily influenced by jazz, folk and literature and was far from limited to 'classically trained' (which often seems to mean 'had music lessons at school') children of wealthy parents.

My goal in this book is not to change the minds of those who cling nostalgically to such limited perceptions, but to show how Peter Gabriel actively engaged in changing and playing with those ideas from the start, questioning origins, interrogating social norms and criticizing the culture of the day. When the book treats of England, it does so in the guise of mythical Albion, and looks to enrich our understanding of a moment in recent history when those myths were in transformation, as we hear, sometimes clearly, sometimes obliquely, even opaquely, in the music of Gabriel's era of Genesis. For readers in Europe (which does include Britain), such a rethinking of myths of Albion is timely, with Britain's curious decision in June 2016 to leave the European Union, a decision driven by dreams of a great industrial past, a great rural past, a time of full employment, and certainty that anyone outside of the normal 'full' English would from now on remain quiet. Gabriel's tour with Sting ('Rock Paper Scissors') had just started, and Sting reprised the opening two verses of 'Dancing with the Moonlit Knight', whose lyrics describe an England being lost, in the process of *Selling England by the Pound*, the 1973 Genesis album the song had opened. Gabriel himself sang the lines in Edmonton, Canada, on 24 July, the final date of the tour, and this was his first live performance of a Genesis track since 1982. As well as the clear message that both singers thought Britain had made a huge mistake in 'leaving Europe', we can also hear the timeliness of Gabriel's reflections on England and Britain that developed over his time in Genesis.

England acts as a sort of ground for Gabriel, but not one that is a determining explanation for him or for his music. Rather, we need to see Gabriel's career as a succession of different ways of thinking about location. In other words, his work addresses the idea of locatedness: what does it mean to be in a specific place at a given time, to reflect on that time and the changes which inevitably occur? Gabriel's work can be understood as a series of reflections on the 'where' of being – and this includes politics, psychology, philosophy, cultural geography, amused reflection, fear, joy, and the full range of emotional and analytical responses. The situation of an individual, whether Gabriel or one of the narrators or characters in his songs, is always mutating, part of an ongoing process that will never be switched off. In the course of thinking about Gabriel in this way, it began to strike me that this idea of location or even of something like dis-location, of place as something perpetually subject to change and renegotiation, was essential to an understanding of his work. Gabriel could be seen as a sort of explorer of the self in the contemporary world. From that perspective, it also became clear that Gabriel's process of locating himself in the world carried lessons beyond those that applied directly (biographically) to himself or to individual relationships. Many ideas now in vogue, and that have passed from high theory to 'normal' use, could be heard in play in his work, often long before they became standard currency (ideas such as hybridity; the post-colonial rethinking of relations between cultures; critical transnational thinking and practice; and techno-logical networked society and its impact on subjectivity). These ideas are there to be read in the lyrics, but are also expressed in the musical choices, the forms, timbres and routes taken through pieces of music. They are there to be seen in the artwork of albums, in the music videos, on the stage, and in experimental and pioneering multimedia works.

Mythical Albion would be one ground, then, but one that would adjust its meaning over time, meshing in with other elements to make up a Peter Gabriel who would dwell in the global, whose home would shift continually, becoming more layered, more connected all the time; in a significant comment (made in 1989), Gabriel declared that 'I feel much less an Englishman, much more someone who lives on this planet', a statement that informs his career and political outlook.[1] After Albion, I look at Gabriel's fascination with America, particularly New York, as he makes the transition from Genesis to being a solo performer. What is interesting for his listeners is Gabriel as a performer, writer and reflective participant in culture, an interest that cannot be subsumed or overridden by the biographical detail. Maybe a productive way of getting to the core of the artist is through the ways in which the work has related to places, to location in general, and what Gabriel means, at all times, if sometimes unconsciously, about the processes of locatedness.

This is a book about the work, and what we can find in it. In the case of New York, the city is as mythical or mythologized as Albion but signals the potential for the existence of what J. G. Ballard would term myths of the near future. I do not dwell on individual places so much as identify how they are approached: whether the space is perceived as something proximate, left behind, lived in, skirted, depicted, endured. Location is always relational, and only partially geographical. It is a set of meanings built up through webs of interactions, histories and stories. Gabriel's first four solo albums (released between 1977 and 1982) mapped out different modes of subjectivity, tracking the ways an individual relates spatially to others and to his or her self, and how that concern grows to encompass more overtly political or cultural ways of being and living in specific places, or travelling through them. The lyrics and sounds of these albums moved constantly between individual and social contexts and presented a politicized understanding of the world, even if often ambiguously.

The release of *So* in 1986 opened up the prospect of a globalized Gabriel. In tandem with his embrace of non-Western musics and developing of 'world music', he became a worldwide pop star and participated in the spread of u.s.-led global media, exemplified at the time by the American TV music channel MTV. This he did with a critical eye from the start, and his stage performances managed to achieve the necessary epic scale for stadium concerts and also puncture that pomposity with regularity. At each stage of the book I examine how Gabriel's live performances have both partaken of the genre of arena music and played with it, and how he has developed his lyrical conceits and narratives through these critical staging practices.

I discuss the question of world music at several points, through the prism of Gabriel's role as founder of WOMAD (World of Music and Dance), founder of Real World and co-director of its studio, label and concerts, alongside his collaborations with musicians from outside the Western tradition, particularly from Africa. While acknowledging the risk of paternalism in these activities, I return over and over to the question of whether it would really be better not to collaborate, promote, enjoy, participate in something like 'world music', as some critics seem to think. Often this criticism is more revealing of critics' own paternalism and subtle refusal of an 'other' they seek to valorize. The term 'world music' is of course a vexed one, implying universalism *and* a lumping together of highly diverse musics into one non-Western 'melting pot', but it is one that has acquired meaning, so just ignoring it is not an option. What I try to focus on is how Gabriel's own practices of interaction with non-Western musicians and musical styles offer a highly positive, very political and ultimately philosophically satisfying way of thinking about transnational music-making (this despite some of his more universalist pronouncements). Across three chapters that take in ideas on Gabriel and world music, I track how Gabriel became a cultural actor within a world that is actually post-colonial – we no longer live in a world where the West is the dominant or exclusive cultural model, and while theorists have speculated about how this knowledge should influence the behaviour of people from previously imperial nations, I will show that Gabriel's music and political inclinations added up to a genuine global and post-colonial practice. I move then from a consideration of the idea of world music in general, and the issue of appropriation, to a set of reflections on Gabriel's label, Real World, and his collaborations with 'world' musicians. Lastly, I explore how Gabriel's music has acted as a positive model of musical hybridity. I have tried to be fair to prospective criticisms of a Western musician somehow exploiting others, and in so doing have almost always found Gabriel to be a step ahead of those problems, precisely because of the centrality of ideas of location and dis-location.

Later chapters explore how Gabriel has participated in contemporary, globalized identity formation (how individuals and cultures develop as part of technological and economic globalization) and world processing (the way in which the 'globalized' world has been understood), such that he has engaged in digital culture in ways that have been speculative, pragmatic and highly liberal, in line with his own political outlook. His political sensibility was awoken in the late 1970s through an understanding of the South African apartheid regime. Since that time, his key political interests have been in the area of human rights: for over thirty years he has been a highly visible advocate and fund-raiser for Amnesty International. He was also a founder of the Witness initiative, which provides people with means to capture and distribute imagery of human rights abuses. Technology has not so much moved on from these activities as come round to their mission.

The developments in music-making machinery have had tangible effects on his output, and he in turn has also provided many models for addressing cultural change as experienced in networks, through heightened connectivity – for example by transforming *Witness* into an online distribution platform. But connectedness is not only a force for political good. It has been exposed in recent years as a means of extreme surveillance and also dubious state intervention, and Gabriel's contribution to the film *Snowden* (2016), directed by Oliver Stone, brings that out with crisp directness. In Gabriel's track for the film, 'The Veil', he outlines Edward Snowden's place outside society, as an exemplar of us all, living as we do in fast-networked systems. The world is data, and people are stripped down into algorithmic micro-gestures. Luckily, we are mostly not worth locating on a map. But Snowden set about revealing the massive u.s. 'oversight' of encoded interactions, and in so doing stepped outside politically recognized physical place entirely, and then sought a type of asylum in Russia. For Gabriel, Snowden is not just someone who exposes the actions of the world's biggest rogue state, but is also a paradigmatic subject of the future, a technologized future that has been on Gabriel's mind since the early solo albums. Technology is always about our place in the world, in how we connect to it – and for Gabriel, it carries a utopian potential and the threat of danger. These currents run through his work and this book. Ultimately, Gabriel moves to critically reconnect global and local in order to think about where he is, where he finds himself, or indeed where he develops, within and across nodes and media connectors.

Finally, I think about his returns to earlier Peter Gabriels, in his work since 2010, and to how his rethinking of his oeuvre has led to a sense of home that has questioned what the idea of home is, such that it is always a different place to which he returns, as if for the first time, every time. This phase has been one of covers, of orchestral reimaginings, of commissioning others to reinterpret his songs – all this just after revisiting the Genesis material to which he contributed so strongly, for the *Genesis 1970–75* box set (in 2008) and while reshaping the album *So* for its 25th Anniversary Deluxe Box Set configuration (2012). Most recently, all of his solo albums have been remastered, doubled in vinyl form, constituting one more return to an uncanny starting point for a continual process of locating and dis-locating. Just as Peter Gabriel seemed set to spiral in upon himself indefinitely, caught forever in a wager on rock or paper or scissors, new material appeared, albeit not in album form but in the shape of the standalone tracks 'I'm Amazing', about Muhammad Ali, and 'The Veil'. The dis-location continues. The reflection on global culture, and how we live it, will not let Gabriel go. In the world he dwells; involved, net-worked – a global citizen.

1 ALBION

The Domesday Book of 1086 lists a village, Cebeham, in what is now the county of Surrey, just south of London. This long-lived rural town, now named Chobham, has no epic tale to tell, and does not nestle in leafy or mountainous splendour. Instead, like much of the English countryside, it has a reasonably autonomous existence amid fields enclosed over the intervening centuries. It never grew vastly in scale or population, it is something of an Everyman village, and it was where Peter Gabriel was born and lived his early years. More specifically, he grew up on Deep Pool Farm, Coxhill, just outside of Chobham. This would be the first of the potentially significant non-urban locations in Gabriel's early life. The second has a much higher profile, another location at the border of a large village or small town. This time, the place is Charterhouse School, the town Godalming, to which the school decamped in 1872. It was in this school that Genesis formed, with the original line-up of Peter Gabriel, Tony Banks, Anthony Phillips, Mike Rutherford and Chris Stewart all being pupils at the school. It was also there that alumnus Jonathan King 'discovered' them and began the process of piecing together the band's first album, *From Genesis to Revelation*, released in 1969. The third of these formative places is another building, a house called Christmas Cottage, and like the other two places, also in Surrey. This cottage was owned by Richard Macphail's parents and was lent for a period of several months to the band. Macphail acted as the band's organizer and took advantage of his parents losing interest in their holiday home to house the band for rehearsing and recording. This was in late 1969 and would lead Genesis to kick-start their career after a disappointing and rather character-less first outing, and to stretch out their songs into what would become their first work as a progressive rock band, the 1970 album *Trespass*.

The story begins with these three potentially formative places, and it would be tempting to read much of Gabriel-era Genesis's lyrical and musical leanings into these settings. While it is hard not to ascribe any influence to them, what is much more of interest is how the band incorporated the places into their music and songs. It would be perverse to attribute the entire 'early' period of the band (1967–75) to a set of determinations about well-heeled country gentlefolk, and yet this has been the dominant popular narrative, in ignorance of much of the biting and critical lyrical drive provided by Gabriel, which he honed over this period. In short, knowing of these places, these sites of his early life, tells us very little. It is much more interesting to look at how the English countryside and its varied societies are refracted through the light of Genesis's actual songs, rather than overdetermining their content, purpose or concerns from a hasty class dogmatism. There is nothing mysterious about those middle-class origins – they were on show from the beginning – but at the same time Genesis would increasingly become part of a shared critical tradition, more visible in 1960s surreal British comedy. Even allowing for the possibility that the group's shared origin, in the shape of one of class-ridden Britain's most exclusive fee-paying schools, might limit the possibility of Genesis being able to express the suffering of the oppressed and exploited, we have to note that very few musicians active in the late 1960s or 1970s did that. Far from being shaped by the school, they moulded themselves against it, with Daryl Easlea noting that

'Gabriel and Banks were united in their distaste for the school'
and reacted against its conservatism and tolerance for bullying.[1]
What is not limited is the capacity of Genesis to tell us about
huge swathes of English life, whether in terms of the past, or
myth, or of the present of the countryside, or the growing sub-
urbs, or the meaning of the city as an all-encompassing world,
perhaps not seen so clearly from within.

British society was in flux in the 1960s, with the most obvious sign being The Beatles and the cultural change that they
represented, taking shape in the 'Swinging Sixties'. One part of
the story is of Britain opening up, becoming more progressive
in outlook and slowly losing its entrenched respect for hierarchy.
Musically, certainly, there was an explosion of variety and innovation, with psychedelia, folk music, jazz and progressive rock all
emerging as significant forms. The latter, which would reach its

Godalming, home of Charterhouse School, where the founding members of Genesis met.

commercial zenith in the early and mid-1970s, was where Genesis were located, with many of the genre's trademarks present in their music: long-form songs, songs based on narrative and musical development rather than repetition, complex instrumentation, and the use of non-rock instruments and styles.

For all the commercial and critical impact of the new musics, fashion and live music scenes, many, perhaps the vast majority, of its citizens lived out a different period of very little change, as conservatism and traditional class structures did not break down in any significant way.[2] Despite this, massive change was occurring. Anti-colonial struggles in the colonies led to the independence of many countries. Britain in the 1960s was only slowly emerging from a long period of austerity and lagging behind the economic progress of many of its competitors. Consumerism, rock 'n' roll, immigration and debates about the worth and morality of having a nuclear missile deterrent were changing the cultural landscape. The enduring class divisions of Britain – with 'old money' aristocracy, middle classes and industrial working classes – were defined to the point of segregation. The class borderlines were represented in the fight between trades unions and employers, and between the Conservative and Labour parties, the two main political parties of the time, and people felt their identity to be heavily structured by class expectations. The system may have been slow to change, but criticism of it was something new, and did represent a dramatic change – and Genesis would come into being towards the end of a decade that had witnessed not just hints of social change, but also the irreverence of the 'satire boom' and best-selling books about class by Richard Hoggart and Raymond Williams, and despite their very clear class 'origins', the group participated fully in the new articulation of resistance to conservative morality, class roles, religion and tortuous levels of respect for authority.

With this shifting bedrock of conflict came another source of unease or utopianism, depending on one's point of view, and this was the modernization of Britain, which was taking physical form in modernist mass housing. Britain witnessed massive rebuilding in the wake of the bombing of the Second World War and the subsequent period of 'making do'. By the late 1950s, huge swathes of urban land were empty and/or derelict, while many lived in slum conditions. Historian David Kynaston takes this rebuilding to be at the heart of the wider changes then happening, and shows that every city would have its modernist housing, new roads, new precincts for shopping.[3] The concerns about this rebuilding would inform Gabriel's lyric-writing and narratives on Genesis's albums *Foxtrot* (1972) and *Selling England by the Pound* (1973).

In parallel to this social and urban progress (as it was seen at the time) was a vindication of more traditional values and arts. The poet John Betjeman was a vocal supporter of historic buildings threatened with demolition, and Britain witnessed something of a 'folk revival' in the 1950s and '60s. This phenomenon can clearly be heard in the second and third of Genesis's albums, *Trespass* (1970) and *Nursery Cryme* (1971). It can be heard musically, but also lyrically, as many of the themes concern rural culture, mythical settings, agrarian societies and timeless themes of love, murder, quests and the valorization of stability over change. However, the folk revival was darker and more critical than this, and so were Genesis, particularly Gabriel, so the listener will hear also of transgression, metamorphosis, anarchist rebellion, and of the strangeness to be found in apparently known, predictable worlds and situations.

From album to album, Gabriel gradually developed a vocal and lyrical style that could convey all of the complexity of a culture that was built on its valorization of tradition yet racing forward in many directions. This style involved dramatic changes in tone, subject-matter, imagery, in order to reveal, analyse, criticize and play with the ideas of British, particularly English, culture, both of the time and throughout history. For that reason, we should regard Gabriel as part of a lineage of English artist-critics who have become part of the mainstream, or seem to have been part of it for ever, with William Blake as the paradigm of this type of critical expression. Gabriel, like the leading Pop artists in Britain in the 1950s and '60s (Eduardo Paolozzi, Peter Blake, Richard Hamilton), used a type of surrealism to mould a complex picture of England's dreaming (as John Lydon, a later musical visionary, would have it).

On the first two albums that Genesis made, there was very little sign of the analytical surrealism that would, in a short time, become their trademark. The lyrics were group-written, with Gabriel taking over this role bit by bit as the first half of the 1970s wore on. The music began to stretch out on *Trespass*, but it would be the next three albums, *Nursery Cryme*, *Foxtrot* and *Selling England by the Pound*, that really illustrated how Genesis, and particularly Gabriel, came to articulate a set of positions and commentaries on the Britain of the time as a kind of cracked mirror of old Albion, an Albion not so much gentle, fair and heroic but one riven by conflict, foolishness, oddness and creative ways out of encroaching conformity. The first two albums were tentative in this regard, but the leap from first to second was still highly significant, and already in *Trespass*, a dark vision of mythical England started to unfold, in line with various other new musics and revivals in a continuum identified by Rob Young in *Electric Eden* (2010) as extending from its first flourish in the 1960s right through to the present day.[4] While Genesis had little to do with the claims for 'authentic' music present in folk revivals of the time, it is my view that their music from *Trespass* onward sprang from the same sources, the same period's outlook on the 'state of the nation', and that Genesis ultimately advanced a much more rigorous and inventive take on myths of England and its country-sides and towns than many of the supposedly faithful renderings of 'folk' music that sprang up in the 1960s, in the second wave of folk revival.

None of this attitude, though, was present on *From Genesis to Revelation*. By the time it was released, the band had moved on from its folk-pop styling and predictable structures and was exploring longer-form songs and preparing the Christmas Cottage sojourn. The band essentially 'disowned the album altogether and insisted that *Trespass* should be treated as the first Genesis album', notes rock critic Bob Carruthers.[5] Jonathan King first met the group when it was comprised of Banks, Gabriel, Rutherford, Phillips and Stewart (the drummer who was replaced by John Silver for all but the 'Silent Sun' track on the album). The album was very much a King construction, forming a concept album based on themes from the Bible, in no particularly meaningful sequence. Many of the tracks were linked by the ham-fisted placement of instrumental segments between them, and the songs were then washed in a bath of strings, arranged by Arthur Greenslade. The result was surprisingly bland given the amount of effort put in to try and replicate the commercial success of post-psychedelic pop and the burgeoning field of the conceptually connected album, and in the end 'the group was aghast', writes Easlea.[6] There was very little that was distinctive about the album, only flashes emerging of what would become their style. The lyrics and singing, despite Gabriel's smooth-voiced performance, were as badly construed as the strings (the misguided group choral singing persisted on two of the six tracks that make up *Trespass*).

The songs tried to combine an English whimsy (much better captured elsewhere by, for example, Giles, Giles & Fripp or the Moody Blues, let alone by the early Pink Floyd or The Kinks) in the choruses, with an inoffensive, mildly soulful versifying. King seemed to be attempting a fusion between American and English styles, based on what was selling well, and then larded it with the

strings as easy listening markers of 'classiness', an early version of
homogenized music doing whatever the opposite is of transcending
place.

Trespass is something else entirely. The sessions in the cottage
led to the adoption of twelve-string acoustic guitars, a vital part
of Genesis's reinvention of the pastoral sound. The drummer also
changed, with John Mayhew providing the percussion this time.
The combination of added power and acoustic instrumentation
was perhaps driven by the band's formative encounter with King
Crimson's debut album, *In the Court of the Crimson King* (1969),
which Gabriel described as 'doing the things we wanted to, but so
much bigger and better'.[7] The soundworld of *Trespass* was much
more heavily composed than that of *From Genesis to Revelation*,
and more purposeful in its combinations. Elegant passages of
guitars, keyboards and flute enwrapped tales from a parallel
mythical land, acting as texture and atmosphere as well as melodic
and harmonic structure. The instrumentation Genesis opted for
went beyond standard rock instrumentation, and they used the
studio to develop already rich textures into evocatively rich sound
combinations designed to take the listener out of time. This new
Genesis, both more ethereal and earthy, began to incorporate
ideas of place, history and reflections on England.

Trespass is an album characterized by movement: into and out
of rules, across borders and fences. The conceit of crossing a line,
the transgression of the trespass, informed the entire album, in
lyrical content, the presentation of those lyrics and the changing
musical sections. Musically and vocally, Genesis worked as a
whole to create sequences of changing moods, in order to capture
narrative drive and also to provide an involved perspective. So,
for example, Gabriel's voice changes dramatically in the course
of individual songs, from straight singing to whispering and
shouting, capturing, above all, yearning and suppressed violence
– the keys to transgressive behaviour in mythical stories that are

designed to transcend time – in a bid to realize his vision of the band as what he described as 'sad romantics'.[8] This instructive phrase gives us a very clear sense of how Gabriel and Genesis saw themselves, and how they tried to address connections to nature, the world, society, individuals. The Romantic movement had looked to a mythical Nature for inspiration, and also tried to rival the great artists of all times, of any historical period, who had reached beyond the mundane and proximate world to address the 'big questions' of life, death and the universe. Gabriel's qualifying addition of 'sad' means that the yearning and melancholic troupe of 'romantics' of Genesis would not be looking to be heroic conquerors of the world, but would instead adopt the role of world-weary, gentle seekers after truth and meaning.

Although Genesis were yet to put their own stamp on the myths of countryside, of heroic figures, of events in distant lands, their songs already demonstrated a knowing mobilization of a generic mythical thinking or storytelling, as opposed to trying to capture an existing myth or recreate music from other times. There are plenty of references to established cultural myths in the course of *Trespass*, but the album occupies a space that is not quite inside any specific mythical realm, as instead it looks on to myths from the (trespassed) border, observing, learning, moulding and remoulding. In short, myth becomes content, the subject-matter, and not just a story to be consumed.

Genesis had already begun to expand their conception of what a song should do, as can be heard on 'Genesis Plays Jackson', the suite that appears on the 'extras' CD in the *Genesis 1970–1975* box, recorded early in 1970. The BBC had approached Genesis to provide a soundtrack to a film about the British painter Michael Jackson, and Gabriel noted they took 'the chance to test out a lot of the musical ideas we were exploring at the time'.[9] While Gabriel was pleased at this aspect, he was less than happy with the vocals, which he described as '[a lot of it] undeveloped and out of

tune, merely a sketch for ideas'.[10] Gabriel was right to identify it as
a sketch, but it represented a test for longer-form pieces and dis-
crete musical ideas – elements would appear on *Trespass*, *Nursery
Cryme* and even *The Lamb Lies Down on Broadway* (1974) – leading
Tony Banks to concur that the exercise was a valuable experiment.[11] Musically, the players created a set of pieces that alternate
between aggressively electric sections full of attack, and other sections where acoustic instruments and electric take a more sedate
path in combination. As well as the actual sequences that would
crop up in later songs, the overall approach to instrumentation
and extended form would feed into the later albums. For Gabriel
himself, that was what was worth retaining, as opposed to any
of his own vocal interventions, which were limited. In addition,
the suite was the band's first experience of matching sound and
thematic ideas to visuals – something that would grow to be very
important for them as a unit, but even more so for Gabriel, who
would go on to develop a significant visual presence onstage and
introduce the epic visuals for the concerts of *The Lamb Lies Down
on Broadway*. Later still, he would make complete soundtracks for
Birdy (1985), *The Last Temptation of Christ* (1988) and *Rabbit-proof
Fence* (2002), and standalone tracks for many other films.

Along with many of their peers in progressive rock, Genesis
were looking to broaden the range of what a rock group could
do. At this stage, this was through the medium of instrumentation and a hinting at a lost (yet only ever retrospective and
imagined) music of the past. Without any conscious mission to be
part of folk music revivals, it is clear that a key part of the material
for these imagined otherworlds would take a misty old England
for some of its cues.

This was not an England where the toiling classes, or even the
economic and social realities of wealthier sections of society, were
shown or heard. For that reason, *Trespass* fell into the category
of abstraction with regard to 'country living', as identified by

Raymond Williams with regard to the eighteenth-century portrayals of country living in literature: 'The English landowning class,
which had changed itself in changing its world, was idealised
and displaced into an historical contrast with its real activities.'[12]
Nonetheless, the title is not insignificant: the transgressive nature
of what lies outside a timeless and tale-drenched land is identified
before we even hear the album (in non-digital form at least). Peter
Whitehead's cover depicts a Renaissance couple overseeing the
land from the sanctity of their redoubt against the realities of the
world beyond. But they are located precisely on the threshold,
and this indicates that they are not necessarily acting within the
rules of their society. Whatever the intent of these illustrated
characters, a knife slashes extra-diegetically: that is, Whitehead
illustrates a realistic, three-dimensional, photorealist knife slicing
through the image. Trespass is outside, not a breaking-in but a
breaking-free of rules, of hidebound society. It is also the moment
of breaking of the alienation created by the illusion of the world
in the underlying drawing. The music of the album is also divided:
the first five tracks tell their tales, structure and inhabit worlds
outside everyday activity of any sort, and echo Romantic visions
of humanity dwelling in nature, the big questions of meaning,
faith and emotion rearing up periodically in the encounter. But
the final track, 'The Knife', inhabits a different world just as much
as Whitehead's meta-knife does on the cover, and shows the
power of the breaking of old models of old England.

Gabriel's voice is the first sound on the album, calling out
the title line of 'Looking for Someone', a song featuring a quest,
uncertainty, travel and the question of a search itself, as the
title suggests. The song in fact suggests something other than a
targeted search of a lost individual, and more than a search for a
love interest. What seems lost is in fact the narrator, and perhaps,
by association, the places that he travels through (which are kept
vague). The narrator may be lost but lives in a time of people

offering easy solutions, ways into the spiritual that may mislead. Verse two tells of the dictates of 'proper' society, a set of rules waved aside by the narrator. Then the music changes, softens, and quiet vocals talk of nature. Verse three is also about being adrift precisely because society attempts to channel and limit an individual's behaviour. By the close, an increasingly assertive Gabriel shouts to be left alone, and in finding this solitude, free from systems of rule, social expectation and faddish alternatives, he is free to declare his identity as that which remains once those shackles have been thrown off. In so doing, he is ready not to abandon society but to join in on his own terms. While the lyrics appear to eschew a quest, the narrator is searching in order to find something elusive, and proceeds through a series of rejections. The musical progression suggests shifting sands on the path to self-realization. The verses fill with electric guitar and drums as they build up from keyboard and vocals, the choruses (the space of self-realization) likewise, but there is a significant calming moment around the middle of the chorus where nature appears, acting as a glade, a clearing. Following the second chorus, with its valuing of a friend (or society) who does not judge the narrator, is a section of purely musical development, signifying potential flight as it speeds up, and the electric guitar break signals the individual breaking free (this returns to close the track). This cuts into a flute-dominated section, reiterating the vocal melody of the verses, thereby showing the narrator assuming control of his actions, despite social pressure to conform.

Although all the lyrics were written collectively by the band, Gabriel's vocal performance of them was central to conveying their meaning, and the dynamism of his presentation transmuted a simple countercultural statement into something deeper and more personal, through explicitly formal means of vocal technique, 'an expressive hoarseness but mostly steeped throughout in a desperate romanticism'.[13] In this sense, too, of a knowing manipulation of form as opposed to an attempt at 'simple' authenticity, Genesis were a long way from any folk revivals, including from the pitfalls of such activity. Gabriel's flute playing ensured that the vocal parts were not simply adrift in the growing expanses of music but were swerved into the musical melody. Looking for place in this song seems perverse, and I have no intention of flensing every song Gabriel has featured on for such reference, but the oddity of the two references in 'Looking for Someone' merit attention, if only to draw attention to the already rippled surface of Albion's land that Genesis were producing. Those two places are 'Damascus' and 'the subway', in succeeding lines. The subway is the strange reference here, with the narrator not only in an underground transit system but one used in North America (hinting ahead to *The Lamb Lies Down on Broadway*). Gabriel's interest in soul music was leading him to look outside English reference points (later he would say to Paul Morley, 'I felt I could repress the middle class English person with soul music'[14]), but the subway could also signal the spread of American commercial power (marketing is the issue in that verse). More interestingly, the reference can indicate how English culture, or any culture when looking at itself, or for itself, has to acknowledge its others – its neighbouring cultures and those it sees as distant in outlook. Damascus, in the Christian Bible, stands for conversion, with the 'road to Damascus' now a widely held trope indicating a life-changing event. But unlike Saul (later St Paul), Gabriel's narrator does not discover God. In fact, Damascus is a potential for future change, something maintained specifically as potential, but unlikely to occur, as he moves on into the self-realization of the second chorus and in the end returns to a new self.

Each song on *Trespass* has its moments of light and dark, and regular sections of plucked and strummed twelve-string and acoustic guitar, in a conscious move away from the rock guitar and hinting at a uchronic Tudor music genre. Other sections take a full group rock dynamic, but still defamiliarize this approach through changing time signatures and a refusal to stay still and use repetition. In this sense, Genesis also tried to echo the classical sonata form, or more accurately, 'classical' music since Romanticism. The non-repetition clarifies narrative development, and as most of the tracks feature or conclude with returns to opening motifs, they also offer reassurance and 'resolution'.

'The Knife' is more monomaniacal, launching directly with its almost military keyboard-led band riff, soon joined by Gabriel's syncopated vocal lines. Gabriel again varies his tone through the course of the song, but never uses the measured whisper that features so often elsewhere. Instead, he expands upward in volume, in aggression, and even outward, through the use of effects on his voice – and as with Greg Lake on King Crimson's '21st Century Schizoid Man' – this harshening signals war. The track proposes a complex take on the use of political violence, rapidly changing into something less than positive, but never losing the sense that violence may be necessary (Max Bell wrote that the song was in fact 'a send-up of revolutionary attitudes'[15]). In the opening verses, the narrator takes leadership and declares to his listening people the need to fight, for rights, freedom, against oppression. The capitalized 'NOW' is both his call to arms and the choral acceptance of his word, the turning of it into action.

Like the rest of *Trespass*, 'The Knife' happens in some notional land where, as Williams would have had it, 'the social order is seen as part of a wider order; what is now sometimes called a natural order, with metaphysical sanctions'.[16] It also razes that land, emptying the mythical hollows and dales, exposing the human-occupied land as one riven by conflict and where rules can be set aside for gain, moral or otherwise. The countryside and tangential references to myth provided a rich resource for Genesis, and with 'The Knife' a different kind of reaction was elicited from that resource, with its atemporal drift into a sense of timeless, even inevitable struggle (ironically recalling Marx's great story of conflict between a cast of changing classes right up to the glory of the Revolution and the end of all historical time).

From their third album on, Genesis managed to fashion a musical approach that echoed darker traditions in the English past as a way of explicitly addressing contemporary situations and social relations in the 1960s and '70s. In the two folk revivals, the later of which was a key component in the development in the 1960s of progressive rock, it was folk music and folk dance that acted as a prism for the ideas of Englishness, English tradition and music as conduit for an authentic life outside the cities. The first of these revivals began in the late 1890s and extended as late as the 1930s (an alternative would be to see one long yet changing continuum of revival, as Georgina Boyes does in *The Imagined Village*[17]); the second began in the 1950s and extended into and informed British psychedelia, beat, progressive rock and folk rock. There are differences between the two revivals: the first was entirely dominated by collectors, the most renowned of whom would not only set the agenda for the terms of revival, but also claimed that their terms were always already in the tradition. Without reducing a broad revival to its key names, we can identify Cecil Sharp, Ralph Vaughan Williams and Mary Neal as central to the project of redefining the role of traditional cultural practice around the turn of the twentieth century. Boyes convincingly identifies the many curious ideological twists and turns and power dynamics, particularly of the first phase. If we condense the second revival into its 'leaders', then we see the influence of audio-anthropologist Alan Lomax, folk singer Ewan MacColl and latter-day collector A. L. 'Bert' Lloyd as the drivers of a more savvy, leftist conception of folk that knew itself to be about renewal as well as maintenance.

The second revival, though, was much broader, and just as Sharp's and Vaughan Williams's ideas became codified in writings and collections, the folk revival was also about new genres and category collision. The 'trad' jazz movement and folk both represented British takes on often American phenomena, notably blues, that were seen as authentically rooted styles. Both strands of new music (in the 1950s and on into the early 1960s) took their inspiration from visiting American singers and guitarists, and the two grew together.[18] The link between traditions was based on the idea of a genuine, authentic musical communication – which today would be thought of in terms of 'roots' music – being a fundamentally shared method of expression of social being, despite formal musical differences. Whereas 'the definition of folk was caught up in the first revival period with a bucolic imagination of England', the second was about how England related to a world beyond, and how it helped refocus attention on to the use of tradition.[19] The later revival was far from being exclusively an English phenomenon, with Scotland in particular leading a massive folk boom.

This second revival was one of the channels into the longer-form lyrical and musical explorations that Genesis and many other bands took in the early 1970s. Even an early album such as *Trespass* was an attempt to elude the dogmatic idea of recovering a true local music, and the later albums escaped the limited notions of Englishness that would reinforce hegemonic values (as identified by Williams, Boyes, Trish Winter and Simon Keegan-Phipps) in favour of a much more mobile, critical and knowingly arch Englishness that partook of the late flowering of surrealism in Britain in the guise of Pop art and comedy from *The Goon Show*, through *Hancock's Half Hour*, and into the conformism-shredding of *Beyond the Fringe*, *That Was the Week That Was* and *Monty Python's Flying Circus*. Radio had even had its own debunking of folk in the shape of Kenneth Williams's Rambling Syd Rumpo on *Round the Horne*. The meek austerity of post-war Britain was being replaced, argued Prime Minister Harold Wilson on 1 October 1963, by the 'white heat' of a revolution combining socialism and science. Instead, Britain had a musical revolution, somewhat supplanting traditionally defined social change; but still, the immediate background for most people was not swinging London, nor was it the village dance. It was urban, industrial and rigidly conformist. For all the social critique provided by the generation of musicians starting out in the 1960s, it would take the extra push of refusal that defined punk to finally turn British conformity into the surreal joke it already was.

With *Nursery Cryme*, Gabriel and Genesis turned the screw another notch on Merrie Olde England, home of the familiar, and were 'putting more humour and more subversion into the music', said Gabriel.[20] The cover, again by Whitehead, shows an endless striated lawn where characters that bring together Lewis Carroll and early surrealism play croquet with heads, glide on roller skates or wander the banded grass in the distance. The cover is Whitehead's interpretation of the opening track, 'The Musical Box', which launches the theme of nursery rhyme in its referencing of 'Old King Cole'. According to the story that accompanies the lyrics, the song announces the return of a recently beheaded Henry Hamilton-Smythe, pleading to rejoin his decapitator, Cynthia Jane de Blaise-William. There is more story, and the use of and comment on the traditional children's song is transplanted by Gabriel into the middle of the 'Musical Box' song. The preceding, more musically pastoral part talks of a kingdom that is fading from the sight of the dead monarch (Henry, in the dying and shrinking shape of his avatar King Cole). As Henry/Cole begins to die for a second time, the closing section emerges from a frenetic band break. Gabriel's voice is near to the microphone, a sinister, proximate figure in search of the 'lady'. Where this song notes the passing of a king, the fading of a kingdom (at least from sight), the second song, 'For Absent Friends', seems to suggest a contrary persistence of the normal – albeit a mythical normal known even in the early 1970s to a diminishing proportion of dwellers in England. It tells the story of an old couple following a weekly ritual of church attendance, and new drummer Phil Collins's steady vocals, absent Gabriel's yearning crescendo that ended 'The Musical Box', suggest a life of solid continuity. The same goes for the plucked and strummed guitar, a signifier of times past. But this tranquillity and stolidity betrays a mounting loss, in the inevitable emptying of the church as the congregation dies out.

'The Return of the Giant Hogweed' is an altogether different take on tale-telling – this time an adventure, where invading plantlife is the star. The titular plant has been brought by explorers to Kew botanical gardens in London, from where it spreads, wreaking revenge for its 'kidnap', and the song closes in the hogweed's voice, declaring its triumph. The music is much less acoustic, and the structure of the song is an ever-changing sequence of micro-melodies and evolving instrumental parts, as is the closing track, 'The Fountain of Salmacis'. 'The Return of the Giant Hogweed' notes very specific places: the field in Russia from which the invasive species came; London; and the gardens of the country as a whole. The alien plant menaces the very core of existing society, imposing a new realm. But this track is not as simple as an expression of fear of the foreigner, or even a critique of that attitude; instead there is a paean to cross-cultural contact over attempts to capture or restrain what is new and different, a kind of multihorticulturalism. So the first half of the album outlines three kinds of passing: kingship, the practices of rural English church society and its members, and also the 'sanctity' of the non-alien homeland.

The album continues with 'Seven Stones', a tale within a tale in that it is a story in the style of Samuel Taylor Coleridge's 'Ancient Mariner', reported by a narrator, such that we get the initial tale, the report, and also the imposition of story type characters, such as the 'old man' who tells the central tale. This central tale is a slender one, but is again a narrative of decline and disappearance, of crafts and of journeys ended. After the syncopation and drive of 'Hogweed', this tune settles into something more straightforward, the band waiting in the wings to blast in after the recurring reference to change without meaning. This somewhat obscure refrain serves to deracinate the uncanny proximate variant of England in the preceding tracks, but it continues the sense of traditional crafts and outlooks passing (the old man is very clearly framed by the narrator as someone he is merely reporting on), so this placelessness can be seen as a parallel to the nineteenth-century craft-utopian William Morris's future vision.[21] Having announced the framing device, this side continues with its settings of stories through narratorial prisms. 'Harold the Barrel' comes at the listener from different character positions (and strong interaction between Collins and Gabriel), which is something that would feature strongly in Gabriel's lyrics on all the Genesis albums he would be involved with. 'Harold' is a 'Bognor restaurant-owner' who seems to have had a breakdown and waits on a window ledge, intent on suicide. But instead of emphasizing Harold's wrongness, tragedy or redemption, the song highlights the bad faith, inauthentic community and strait-laced nature of a society that does not want to create a fuss, as the media, the police, the mother and the townsfolk end up making him even more of spectacle. As they try to talk him down, the lyrics end with him telling everyone else to take the proverbial running jump. Here, Genesis, and Gabriel in particular, were very close to the comedy of their time. The sense of someone overwhelmed by the constraints of social expectations when those were benevolent but fundamentally misguided or even evil could also be seen in *Fawlty Towers* (first shown in 1975) and *The Fall and Rise of Reginald Perrin* (first series 1976).

Thus far, *Nursery Cryme* offers a strongly geographically located set of stories, conveyed as stories, not as internal

monologues or journalistic reports. It also digs at the traditional
values that an older generation was starting to fear would evap-
orate. The closing two tracks step outside place again and refer
to historical tales – 'Harlequin' takes its lead from the Italian
tragicomic plays of the *commedia dell'arte*, and 'The Fountain of
Salmacis' fuses tales of Hermaphrodite and Salmacis from Greek
legend. 'Harlequin' pursues the linking idea of disappearance,
as guitars fill the track with arpeggios that build a picture slowly,
while the lyrics muse on nature disappearing. The call comes to
recall the harvest, and also children's play. In other words, there
is the possibility that humans and nature can interact in future,
if we hold on to the idea that nature is constant. The music in
fact suggests a tonal and harmonious history safely embedded in
nature – exactly the kind of twee vision bemoaned by Raymond
Williams. However, as it nears its end, 'Harlequin' makes it
clear that although all is not lost, something is currently out of
joint, and so the song does not rest in a completely secure idyll.
Harlequin is the hopeful yet tragic figure, again mirrored in
another important British (and very urban) work of the time,
Michael Moorcock's Jerry Cornelius series (first volume, *The Final
Programme*, 1968), where the central character was often in danger
of losing all around him, creating disaster accidentally, or just not
knowing who or where he is.[22]

The tales of *Nursery Cryme*, including 'Fountain of Salmacis',
were in fact highly specific as a collection of tales that made sense
in the now of 1971, the 'now' of 'The Knife', or the 'now' that
returns over and over to conclude 'The Musical Box'. Past and
mythical stories are always of a here and now, and I do not say
that to enforce a contextual determinism on Genesis. Rather I
want to say that Gabriel and Genesis identified that here and now
was where all myths would live or die, and that the England of
their time was and is meaningfully present within the songs. On
the following year's release, *Foxtrot*, this was strengthened by a

heightened musical contribution to the critical re-presentation of ideas of England, and reached a sort of apotheosis in 'Supper's Ready'.

Several of the tracks on *Foxtrot* continued the now familiar Genesis strategy of shifting between mythical, historical and mundane registers, while the instrumentation was divided between more acoustic and/or pastoral sections, meditative connecting parts and more rigorous full band sections, and Gabriel's voice covered a huge span of tones, affects and grains. The overall feel of these tracks is of explorations far from the everyday, the grounded, the historically mythical, even if they pursue large-scale questions of passing time, Earth's status in the universe, humanity's fate, the relation between the material, ideal and ethereal, and mirror dreams of power in the mode of the *vanitas*. But alongside the rich, even fulsome exploration of Albion in 'Supper's Ready', there is also the futurebound tale of 'Get 'Em Out by Friday', which moves between the rent racketeers of the present to soul and body control in a far future built on the world of today.

This track details the suspect practices of landlords in 1970s Britain, inspired by the notorious slum landlord Peter Rachman, whose name became a byword for maximizing profit from rental accommodation while barely bothering to keep the buildings standing, let alone attend to tenants' needs. The title summons up the spectre of a gang of hoodlums contracted to remove troublesome tenants – where trouble can be construed as not being willing to pay arbitrary increases on rent payments. On one side stand Mr Pebble, developer extraordinaire, and Mr Hall, thug. Mrs Barrow and Mary are on the other, and are called upon to leave, to get out, even though they have agreed to a prior rent increase and foolishly thought this would protect their tenancy. Mrs Barrow is voiced gently as a trusting innocent by Gabriel, unable to believe what she sees. She is threatened several times and is stripped of her home. For the villainous developers, Gabriel uses a gleeful, boisterous voice to deliver menaces, demands and dishonest negotiations. In the future (in the song), such practices are extended to controlling the height of occupants so as to fit more dwellings in high-rise apartment blocks. The future part comes after a pastoral, instrumental passage where guitar, flute and keyboards play reflectively and slowly to indicate the passage of time. This then cedes to the shouted declaration about the new rules mentioned above, followed by a chirpy statement from a character listed as 'Joe Ordinary in Local Puborama' (although condescendingly named, the 'ordinary fellow' rationally expresses sadness at the new restrictions).

Mrs Barrow offers to pay double the rent to stay in the property, but Mr Hall has a counter-offer – £400 and a new abode. As she concedes to leave, to live in Harlow, Mrs Barrow finds that the rent on the new place is also about to go up. Not for the first time, Gabriel was extrapolating a contemporary situation into a larger narrative, complete with future dystopia, and even in the pastoral 'passage of time' section Gabriel's flute marked melancholic passing – the refrain of which was continued by the keyboards into the future – gardens turning to weeds amid car parks. The story, though, was deeply contemporary, addressing the plight of post-war working-class people amid the shoddy rebuilding and tenancy rackets of the time. Although the song focused on private developers, vast numbers were turfed out of their homes by public authorities too, in order to make way for council-run tower blocks and low-rise estates. The compulsory purchase order saw to those who owned their property, and council tenants in their multiple thousands were simply moved. On the other hand, as John Grindrod points out in *Concretopia*, for many people, new towns, new estates, concrete, ultra-modern, practical designs, were perceived as being full of potential, and for a while in the 1950s and much of the 1960s, a Britain oddly converted in a flash to tenets of modernist design seemed in the grip of a planning utopia.[23] By the 1970s this was unravelling, as buildings and communities began to fail, creating pockets of isolated yet heavily populated dwelling zones that were the opposite of towns. In 'Get 'Em Out by Friday' Gabriel highlighted the dependency, hope and accepting nature of the renting population of Britain – financially and geographically hemmed in by the new world ostensibly designed to liberate their creative and communal potentials.

The choice of location was no accident – Harlow, site of current and future high-rise experimentation and inequitable pricing in the song, was one of the post-war designated 'new towns' (in the New Towns Act 1946). Like Chobham, it too had featured in the Domesday Book, but now it turned to a concrete, planned, condensed massification for its future. In the 1970s this was all still happening, as buildings poured into solid form in estates, around the heavy-set girder of the new centre. So rather than just being a song complaining about bad people exploiting good people, this track explored the multifaceted, if ultimately flawed, utopia that was growing in physical, built reality in the southern English satellite town of Harlow. Like Gabriel's vision of the future block that is part of an ever-larger scheme, the satellite towns were just that – designed to capture, house and discipline surplus Londoners, with the dual promise of being outside the city and retaining all the benefits of city culture. Or the worst parts of a city, having little by way of cities' usual compensations. As time passes from the moment planners dreamed of a concreted future and buildings, estates and cities that visually resembled an experiment in Soviet-style construction, it seems ever odder that anyone thought this was a good idea, yet the happier precedents of the garden cities, and parallel success of some new towns, cannot protect the more concrete and heavily planned towns from falling into the realm of unlikely mythical spaces, to be mourned not for their passing but for their existence. 'Get 'Em Out by Friday' is rare in that Gabriel offers no positive side to the newly mythified new town of Harlow and the wider phenomena it represented. There is no charm, only the quenching of Mrs Barrow's goodwill. Gabriel had put his finger on a turning point – the satirical chiding of Britain was to turn into the social unrest of the 1970s and '80s.

The epic 'Supper's Ready' seems almost more traditional in light of this contextualization of 'Get 'Em Out by Friday', but the latter needs to be seen as informing the former. 'Supper's Ready' raises the mundane to the heroic, but also questions what that transition might mean when that heroic mundanity is all that is left. The raising of the question of utopia, of critical utopia, is clear in the closing line's reference to heading to the 'New Jerusalem'. This is a direct reference to William Blake's 'outsider', early nineteenth-century vision in *Jerusalem* of a renovated dream of a future paradise in England. Gabriel was also consciously using the Christian Bible, stating that 'there is a line in Revelations [the last book of Christian writings known as the New Testament, and a vision of the Apocalypse] which says "this supper of the mighty one".'[24] In 'Supper's Ready', the journey has humbler beginnings, starting with a walk to the television, from which, or possibly despite which (as the TV is turned off), this post-war New Town Jerusalem arises. Although writers have noted the combination of mundane and mythic in the song, the contrast between acoustic and electric, the presence of the Christian Bible and even the 'original' dreamlike visions that inspired Gabriel's lyrics, it is the specific connections between Blake's poem and 'Supper's Ready' that enable a fuller understanding of the song. Even the method matches Blake's visionary approach, as Gabriel 'used the technique of "stream of consciousness" writing where thoughts are allowed to tumble out of the mind', and this included images half-remembered from the biblical end of all things.[25] This reading insists on the parallel locations identified in the song: the existing world, and the possible one that lies ahead through human achievement, along with godly assistance.

'Supper's Ready' is a song of dualities and their overcoming in metamorphosis. The real world is full of harsh contrasts, based on the opposition of real and dream or myth, while the other realm is one where no such borders pertain. The song, like Blake's poem, is not simply one that combines real and dream, but offers categorical differences between them and then breaks them down. This is clear in the first section, 'Lover's Leap', where Gabriel's dual voicing – one in the deeper, more recitative 'chest voice'; another in the more strained, shaped 'head voice' – brings us into the song's world-building.[26] Similarly, section two, 'The Guaranteed Eternal Sanctuary Man', talks of a fireman and a farmer, who tend fire and farm respectively – with the harvest between them. In the predominantly Christian imagery of the track, these surely represent God and the Devil, adversaries combining to reap among the dead (Easlea hears echoes of Enoch Powell stirring up racial tension after his infamous 'Rivers of Blood' speech of April 1968[27]). By the time of melding mutation in the song's conclusion, these

Peter Gabriel performing 'Supper's Ready' with Genesis in 1973.

entities merge, challenging the right of either to imagine himself 'the good one', as 666 (the 'Devil's number') cedes to the seven trumpets of the world's end. As six is always deemed evil, so seven is one of God's numbers. The two have already been shown to be metaphysically linked in the form of the six figures glimpsed out of the window while a seventh lurks nearby, in verse one. As for what this tells us about location, it configures the meaning of apocalypse into a colossal moment of fusion, beyond good and evil – so neither heaven nor hell, and not even this earth as such, but some transformed version of this earth.

We begin in the living room, the domestic interior ('we' are explicitly included in the song's journey, as 'we' is specified in the lyrics, several times, and as 'we' go on, 'we' become aware that Gabriel is acting as lyrical guide to the listener). Outside is a lawn, and beyond that the fading sound of cars. This suburban terrain is a premonition of sanctuary, one that will be progressively unveiled as something inadequate, but also something that contains the occult within it, as the empirical world fades. This fading is a coming to the senses, as identified in the return from somewhere far away, made possible by the switching off of the sanctioned netherworld of television. Comfort has led to an alienating duality. After the second part, which exposes God and the scientist as hucksters, we observe a battle, and on its conclusion witness a scene of repose, also exposed as illusion – the spectacle of peace is only that. After clambering over a mass of dead bodies, we see peaceful fields, nature reborn – a sign of man's travails put in perspective in terms of the planet's ecosystems. In fact, more significantly, we are making a visual mistake, for the tranquil, reflective person we see has been branded, just like bacon. This makes a triple reference to the physical working of human bodies in war, to the supposed similarity of human and pig flesh, and also to the 1970s advertising for Danish bacon, where the word 'Danish' was branded into the fat. So we not only have a critique

of war's supposed justice and just outcomes, but also one of the
foolishness of believing in national identification, as it is just a
form of branding. The observed youth is revealed as Narcissus,
who turns into a flower, caught in the perils of self-satisfaction,
satiety and pride.

From here, metamorphic process fills the song. English references too – to Winston Churchill, prime minister of the country
during the Second World War, and upper-class slang, familiar
from children's stories, revealed in the peculiarity of bricks, eggs
and princes, where both brick and (good) egg signify a reliable and
friendly person. The egg mutates further, symbolizing the potential of the creatures of 'Willow Farm' to breed, grow, travel. But
this farm can make anything, modify anything, in an absurdist-
scientific take on Adam's animal-naming in the Book of Genesis.
This section is broken by a whistle and the instruction to 'all
change', in a caricatural and sonically exact reference to railway
announcements made in Britain, and metamorphosis is brought
back to earth and diverted to another train. From here, the world
of a significant portion of inhabitants of 1970s England flies into a
flux of mums and dads and doings, incidentally revealing a social
gender divide, one that goes away in the fusion of the closing section, 'As Sure as Eggs is Eggs', going beyond alienation, as mums
transmute through mud to become dads (and vice versa).

As the song progresses, Gabriel adopts different vocal
positions to heighten the signification of the lyrics and their
integration with the music (much of which was in place when
the lyrics were written). So the voice travels from the opening
duality, through a mournful tone, into a more shouted section,
giving way in turn to a melancholic calm, into the frantic jollity
of 'Willow Farm', which then turns into music-hall jauntiness.
From here, though, the music becomes more powerful, as
another battle unfolds, one where the border between restrictive
real and open otherspace (dream, myth, utopia) is at stake and

will fall. 'Apocalypse in 9/8', with its off-kilter, keyboard-led march building inexorably, sees a host of mythical creatures and events summoned, like a superhero crossover event, leading into 'apocalypse' as foretold in Revelation. Something strange happens, because to introduce the return of the now much altered sitting room, Gabriel talks of Pythagoras (he of the music of the spheres), who is composing the words of a new song, and not so long after, as fusion reaches its resolution, we hear that there is an angel outside, crying out. Given the earlier references in 'Supper's Ready' to 'The Musical Box' and 'Fountain of Salmacis', it is clear that self-reference is part of Gabriel's purpose. He identifies himself as the prophet, as Blake was, who can transmit the message of utopia to come, to be made flesh, in this land.

'Apocalypse in 9/8' ends with a 'physical', lyrical and musical return to the sitting room, this time with added electric guitar lead line, that resolves the tune of the opening section and draws us into the apocalyptic outcome, which is when our souls are set on fire and all merge, while at the same time coming home. The song closes with the combination of 'home' and 'Jerusalem' in one fused location, as the Lord leads his children into utopia. For Blake, Jerusalem was a utopia that was lost because hidden, and it awaited its uncovering as the true destiny of all humanity. So the sitting room does not have to transform into Jerusalem, because underneath the illusion, it is already there. The illusion falls away and utopia becomes present. There does not seem any doubt, despite the critique of the 'Guaranteed Eternal Sanctuary Man', that Gabriel followed Blake here in attributing the power of bringing people to utopia, and therefore the making of Jerusalem, to some sort of god. But in the fusion of 'Supper's Ready', the borders between human, natural, divine, real and utopia have all melted away. Everyone is a lord, no individual more than any other; every place, every actual place in England (in Blake's poem) is part of Jerusalem as utopia.

At the same time, the listener might also have noticed that we end up where we started, if seemingly transformed – but what if the entire journey was a mediated spectacle, the utopia identifed by naysayers as being a utopian unrealizable dream? The closing section title points both ways: 'As Sure as Eggs is Eggs' reminds us of the growth-generating machine that is the egg, and its power to induce endless mutation in the form of life. But also, the phrase is a truism, a vapid statement along the lines of 'it is what it is.' The 1960s also saw the British government heavily promoting 'the egg' as an ideal healthy snack, breakfast or supper component, fit for a society seemingly in thrall to the 'white heat' of belated modernization. In this case, all that has happened is that 'Supper's Ready' has scrolled through utopian potentials only to realize that love, based in a secure (if porous) house or apartment, is, best of all, a condensation of dream and real. I think that the dualities of the song, combined with the fusing of differences, along with Gabriel's multiple referencing of Blake's 'Jerusalem', mean that both conclusions are in play at once. The music reaches a triumphal conclusion, then dwells in it for the closing minutes, matched by Gabriel's assertive, soaring vocal. Numerous lyrical and musical returns signal that we are in both the material and mythical or higher reality, and that, just as with Blake, both real and utopia must subsist, if they can, in side-by-side fashion, influencing each other rather than one superceding or denying the other.

The early parts of Blake's 'Jerusalem' are full of division, and also the perils of industry and technology, but 'Jerusalem [is] the Emanation of the Giant Albion' (plate 27).[28] For Blake, Albion has lost the run of his kingdom, and recovers the land from poison as the epic unfolds, such that Albion is the whole world, a whole world realizing it has the potential for utopia, because this utopia (Jerusalem) has been hidden away.[29] Blake's vision postulates a time when cities and villages alike will be capable of understanding their true natures, their belonging in 'Jerusalem', and separation will be resolved.[30] Those more familiar with the song 'Jerusalem', Blake's (discarded) preface to his work *Milton, a Poem*, set to music by Hubert Parry over a century later, will have imagined a more bucolic Gabriel, hamstrung by his appurtenance to a fading upper- or middle-class gentry, just as they misread Blake through the prism of that class's appropriation of the song. This appropriation was regularly mocked in *Monty Python's Flying Circus* as a marker of conservative, would-be cultured English herds, and mocked by Gabriel in the subtitle of the closing section of 'Supper's Ready', which trades the phrase 'and did those feet' for 'aching men's feet'. This conservative reading of the preface to *Milton* runs absolutely counter to Blake's revolutionary scrying of the land beneath and around him. Even within that now revered song it should be clear that Blake was wary of the England he saw around him – the 'dark satanic mills' and the explicit statement that the 'green and pleasant land' is not yet Jerusalem are evidence aplenty of the utopia not yet realized.

The links between the hundred-plate poem *Jerusalem* and 'Supper's Ready' are many, yet it is the location of utopia and the kind of place it is that offer the strongest connections. Like Gabriel's lyrics in many Genesis songs, *Jerusalem* refers to many places, places that float between concrete and fabulous realities, whose very existence between the states is the glimmer of utopia – ghostly potential, lost past and hidden present. Blake not only talks of cities and villages in harmony, but also lists many specific locations within Albion's realm (including Ireland, Wales and Scotland, but with England to the fore). The land, or as Gabriel has it in 'Supper's Ready', the soil, is of Albion's realm but the least part. The most important is the realized Jerusalem, which will come into being through the shedding of division, whether sexual, social or economic, and so Blake brings us to the triumphant concluding verses, which resonate vibrantly, like a ghostly kingdom, in the finale of 'Supper's Ready':

All Human Forms identified even Tree Metal Earth & Stone.
all
Human Forms identified, living going forth & returning
wearied
Into the Planetary lives of Years Months Days & Hours
reposing
And then awaking into his Bosom in the Life of Immortality.

And I heard the name of their Emanations they are named
Jerusalem

(Blake, *Jerusalem*, plate 99)

At the end of both visions, the worlds of the quotidian and
the heavenly conjoin – all flesh becomes one, losing apparent
self-identity to join a thoroughly mixed, borderless being, in and
as Jerusalem – as indicated in plate 100 of Blake's poem, where,
just as with the igniting souls of 'Supper's Ready', the entire scene
is of human and divine beings merging through fire.

A new nationalism has appeared in twenty-first-century England,
and this vindication of Englishness rests strongly on Britain's
supposed difference from Europe, with British identity mostly cor-
alled by assertions of Englishness – as witnessed in Albion's Brexit
Tribulation of 2016.[31] When Genesis released *Selling England by the
Pound* in 1973, Britain was caught up in a debate about whether
to join the then European Economic Community (EEC), leading
to rifts inside both major parties of the period (Conservative and
Labour). *Selling England by the Pound* played out another version of
dualism, with the everyday, unnoticed practices of actual Britain
traded against mythical Albion and myths from the world, to
create a subtle, disquieted vision of a Britain headed more and
more into the arms of the gods of commerce.[32]

The album is bookended by a shared lyrical and musical concern, in the opening of both 'Dancing with the Moonlit Knight' and the closing 'Aisle of Plenty': commercial British products are listed and punned upon, illustrating a fall into commodification, particularly in the figure of the supermarket, destroying older models of market exchange and the social interactions and implications that flow from each situation. The supermarket represents the stripping away of social aspects of trading in favour of simple, faceless commerce; and other, more personal, more local forms are implicitly praised by Gabriel as the lost ideal – a fading Jerusalem, even. A deep melancholy infuses the portrait of decay: your golden age to be succeeded by the prospect of eating in fast-food chain Wimpy.[33]

Peter Gabriel dressed as the goddess Britannia, 1973.

The album title suggests the betrayal of Olde England, but this would be an incomplete reading of its intent. The 'pound' of the title refers to both currency and weight (made clear in 'Aisle of Plenty') – so while Britain may have imagined it was being sold down the river, the use of the measure 'the pound' insists on the maintenance of a local tradition, as opposed to the metric system (British currency had only recently changed, in 1971, from imperial to decimal currency divisions). Since the advent of the euro currency in 2002, the pound (in both senses) has been a rallying mechanism for right-wing dreams of a unitary past and present culture. Gabriel challenges this by bringing the reality of Britain, in its self-generated petty commercialism, to light. Elsewhere on the album, Banks and Rutherford play with both classical myth and *The Waste Land* by T. S. Eliot to similar effect on 'The Cinema Show', but the critical edge of the prospect of 'Jerusalem' that filled the bulk of *Foxtrot* is largely pacified on this album with a broader sweep of mountains, greenery, rivers – perhaps holding out for a secret idyll away from city and suburban living.

With 'The Battle of Epping Forest', Gabriel again recasts the Albion of the present day. This story, with music barely less epic than 'Supper's Ready', is a lengthy, character-strewn take on the epic battle – this time between rival gangs, fighting over a pitch for fast-food sales and over 'protection' rights in the 'food trade' that relate to such territory. As the battle unfolds, Gabriel takes up several character voices (as he also does in the more rural 'I Know What I Like', with Gabriel's description of a dark core to be found in the 'therapeutic violence in the act of mowing the lawn'[34]). We could muse on whether he intended this to be an affectionate portrait of various working people and criminals, or whether instead it turns into a patronizing vision that he will never adopt when taking an interest in non-English cultures. But beyond the issue of portraying people outside one's milieu, what the song emphasizes is the prurient interest the Britain of 1973 took in violence, and its glorification of criminal gangs. That this song is about spectacle as part of the contemporary British condition emerges from the oddly strong emphasis on the word 'picnic', which occurs twice, each time repeated three further times. The word is isolated, bringing to an end verses that talk of people enjoying food consumption as the fighting rages, and is stated bluntly, forcefully. The picnic as a mode of vicarious consumption is not restricted to the spectacle of crime, but also to its very core – the countryside, the road, even, becomes leisure. Official parking spots designate views, food is consumed outdoors as if we live in the wild, but it has been foraged from your own larder, and before that, from the supermarket.

Ironically, this picnic ties in to 'I Know What I Like' – with its quasi-surreal take on rural flight to the cities. As the countryside becomes less 'viable' it takes on more scenic interest, and in so doing becomes even less viable, as the 'picnic' expands to take the form of buying holiday homes in villages where local working people cannot afford to live. Genesis, particularly when Gabriel took the lyrical reins, identified vital and subtle changes and problems in the Britain of the time, a Britain that centred on England for mythical ends (and for the more parochial reason of the limits of band's cultural knowledge). 'The Firth of Fifth' nearly takes the listener to the Scottish locations of the Firth of Forth and of Fife, only to eschew them in favour of broad landscape images closer to what Raymond Williams identified as problematic use of the countryside to represent a land cleared of its function, dwelling, economics and culture, even its possibly heroic culture, lost in the broad brush of the picnicking lyricist.

The sequence of Genesis albums from *Trespass* to *Selling England by the Pound* saw Gabriel increasingly taking charge of the lyrics and strongly developing not just the visual and performative identity of the band, but also its way of looking at contemporary life amid wider mythical perspectives. Rather than being limited to the Englishness attributed to the band – wealthy, fee-paying school attending, classically trained, beholden to Anglican Church traditions of thought and song – these were subsumed, even overcome, in the approach that the band forged in their music. The group, under the lyrical leadership of Gabriel, fused ever more epic composition with a strong awareness of social problems, a clear social critique, the prospect of utopias worth aspiring to, and a sense of the country as a location undergoing major change (as always), where the everyday was capable of attaining epic quality and the supposedly timeless, bucolic, pastoral was brought back in touch with its social and historical grounding. But as Gabriel took over the lyric-writing duties, and a significantly larger part of the songwriting, it was not into the heart of England that he went, but to the underground of New York.

2 NEW YORK, NEW YORK

They look behind at every step & believe it is a dream.
Singing. The Sun has left his blackness, & has found a fresher morning
And the fair Moon rejoices in the clear & cloudless night;
For Empire is no more, and now the Lion & Wolf shall cease

William Blake, *America, a Prophecy*, plate 8[1]

In the mid-1970s, New York loomed large in Peter Gabriel's thoughts. The city was both interesting in its own right and able to stand in for American culture. It represented a fizzing and edgy other to the Albion of the early Genesis albums. It was modern, urban, conflicted and spatially complicated. 'What fascinated me about New York,' said Gabriel in January 1975, 'was the speed and aggression of the city.'[2] Beyond the shores and hills of England lay the streets, avenues and subway tracks of a city that stood as future to the heft of Albion's past. That is before we get to the secret rivers, chambers, sluices, corridors of the netherworld found by the protagonist of *The Lamb Lies Down on Broadway*, in Gabriel's sprawling story that unfolds over a double album. Following the subtle pathologizing critiques of mythologized Britain undertaken on the preceding two albums, Gabriel left the shores of Albion behind for 'a fantasy beginning in New York. The central character has a basis of speed and New York is a city of extremes' (as Gabriel described *Lamb* in 1974).[3]

Gabriel's interest in the u.s., and in New York in particular, took shape principally in the setting of events in New York on *Lamb*, but also played a role in marking the end of his engagement with the band. The album's release coincided with the beginning of a North American tour in late 1974, in which Genesis played the album in its entirety, a highly unusual phenomenon at the time (despite being a staple of concerts in the twenty-first century), although Yes had taken the same plunge with their double concept album *Tales from Topographic Oceans* earlier that same year. The *Lamb* tour was the highpoint of Gabriel's control of the band's direction, with all lyrics (except one song) written by Gabriel, costumes designed and worn by him, and visuals that he helped design. This control was the main reason that the album was played in full, as Gabriel conceived the album as forming a coherent whole that could and should be presented as such. Interviewed while on the tour, Gabriel stated that 'the concerts should work more like a film.'[4]

This level of artistic control was also something that was divisive within the band, and it was during the 1974 U.S. tour that Gabriel definitively informed the group he was leaving, having threatened it earlier that year. With Genesis behind him, his new solo career saw him continue the American engagement, with his first solo concerts taking place in the U.S., while his first album and band were heavily inflected by American music and musicians. In short, the *Lamb* album was at the heart of a purposeful and sustained encounter with American culture, with 'the city' at its core and New York its centre, as Gabriel had thought for some time that 'spending time in America might well change our music for the better by making us seem less isolated in our opinions. Soul music excites me more than rock and roll.'[5]

The New York of *Lamb* was as real and/or as mythic as any of the references to 'timeless' culture or to more historicized references to British or English culture developed in depth by Gabriel on *Foxtrot* and *Selling England by the Pound*. In some measure, Gabriel used the same strategies in the *Lamb* period. He explored the crossover between real and imagined, and between reality and myth, and he did that using 'expressive' costumes and stage performance, developing complex narrative through the songs. But where before he had told stories around songs, at tangents to them, now he had a complete double album across which he could develop a story. Not content with that, he wrote a parallel story, printed, on its original release, on the inner part of a gatefold sleeve. Like his lyrics and contiguous tales on previous albums and tours, the narrative of *Lamb* was far from straightforward, but it did track a journey, even if the story veered hither and yon, over and under ground.

The story was certainly convoluted, and not to all of the band members' tastes: 'the actual story is the weakest thing about the album,' said Tony Banks in 2007, while Mike Rutherford (in 2014) reckoned that the story did not really hang together – opinions both have held from the time of the making of the album and unswervingly ever since.[6] The story follows Rael and his brother John on a Moebius (s)trip through the streets, underground passages and symbolic caverns, streams and netherworlds of New York. While the narrative complicates the division between real and mythical New York, the bulk of the journey takes place under the streets, in zones that replicate in a dream-like fashion the world above, with its business, capitalism, class divisions and conflicts and alienation.

Rael is mostly trying to escape the symbolic representations of the problems of the real world city, and is often under threat above ground. Early on, in 'Fly in a Windshield', a mysterious wall descends on Times Square, but nobody notices. This moment is what transports Rael into the underworld of the city, but it is significant that everyone continues their business, faced with a deadly alien intrusion into their landscape, as the vast majority of those who dwell underground are entirely brainwashed into thinking their activities are necessary, when they are actually dictated by some sinister centralized power. 'Cuckoo Cocoon' continues the sense of overlay that Rael experiences, as he imagines himself in a Brooklyn jail, while he is in a cave, underground. Trapped, he notes that it is just like '22nd Street' (the famous early modernist building the Flatiron is at the intersection of 22nd and

Broadway), Gabriel emphasizing throughout the first part of the album (side 1 of 4 in the vinyl version for which the album was conceived) that real and underground map onto each other so that they intertwine. New York has a famous underground travel system, although this does not feature as such in the story of *Lamb*, other than a brief aural glimpse for the lead character when the track 'Anyway' sees Rael confusing a horse with a train sound, showing that the actual subway system is a ghostly parallel to 'his' underworld. But the whole album could be conceived of as a mirror of the subway, or the transit system, that traverses above and under ground, mapping out the city. With those links made between physical New York and its imagined ghostly double, Rael's underworld adventure becomes a metaphorical dissection of modern, urban life driven by capitalism, exclusion and the search for status.

Rael is a Puerto Rican gang member, though Gabriel made the point that he 'spent a lot of time thinking of a name that would owe nothing to any particular nationality . . . and it has no traceable ethnic origins'.[7] The character of John is presented as his imprisoned or captured brother, but by the end seems to have been only the double, or another facet, of Rael. The bulk of the story, as traced in parallel in the lyrics and the written text on the album cover, takes place in a fantastical world underneath the streets of New York, outside time. Rael travels through a series of menacing places and encounters on a journey of self-discovery.

In this story, which only acquires coherence with a patient acceptance of surrealist connections, leaps and juxtapositions, Gabriel moved on from the kind of locations and locatedness seen and heard on the preceding albums. He developed a much more dislocated and unpredictable geography (or topology, where shapes are turned and transformed through different dimensions) within which ideas, symbols and concepts build and unravel. The journey that occurs in the album tracks the movement and shifts in images of place, through the idea that places can shape-shift, can flicker in and out of reality, and can gain or lose meaning to the people who inhabit them or pass through.

The journey takes place in what could be thought of as a mythical midworld – a location that is neither fully fictional nor entirely real, one that traverses physical and psychological spaces – the journey is not merely dreamed or imagined.[8] Other mythological and science-fictional characters punctuate the unwitting quest, as do images of a parallel world that comment on the realities of 1970s urban living/working, living/dying. In interviews conducted in 2007 for the Genesis album remasters, the rest of the band remain chary of the concept and also the effects of Gabriel's lyrical and conceptual takeover. Rutherford has made the point (in 2014) that he was pleased that he and Banks contributed a song ('The Light Dies Down on Broadway', towards the end of the album), so that they 'wouldn't have to live with an album that had "all words by Peter Gabriel" written on it'.[9] Steve Hackett has damned *Lamb* with faint praise in estimating that it would have made 'maybe a great single album'.[10]

Despite the impression they had of ceding control, all four instrumentalists have claimed (in interview in 2007) that some of their best work happened on *Lamb*, as there was space not only to develop instrumental passages through improvisation, but to keep the results and integrate them into the album. Ultimately, while Gabriel considered that 'it's great we went out on such a good piece of work', Collins chose to single out the way in which the band were playing in one room, with Gabriel in another.[11] Echoed by the other members of Genesis, this sense of a growing distance that took on real spatial form would only be increased by the division between Gabriel as actor, director and narrator of the album when played as a whole, with the band feeling trapped into serving the album: Rutherford said, 'we were stuck playing the whole thing' and 'never found playing *The Lamb Lies Down on*

Broadway particularly satisfying', while Banks opined that 'no song really stands out on its own' so it needed to be played as a whole; Collins represented the rest of the band's view about the tour in stating that the 'music was overshadowed by the visuals'.[12]

Meanwhile, events outside Genesis were taking Gabriel further from the democratic band model. First, he had been approached by William Friedkin (director of *The Exorcist*) to develop a film idea with him, and although this came to nothing, it led to Gabriel's first declaration that he was going to leave, opening a breach with the band; second, while recording was going on, his wife Jill gave birth to Anna-Marie, in July 1974.[13] The birth and subsequent period were medically fraught, and Gabriel was travelling, on a sporadic basis, first to Headley Grange in Hampshire, then to Newcastle Emlyn in Wales, in order to piece together the recording. While these locations would fit perfectly to Genesis's late surrealist take on Britain, the preparation of *Lamb* in this combination of circumstances seems to have led to a loss of identification with the project as a whole for most, or even all, of the band members, albeit in very different ways.

With *Lamb*, Gabriel pushed to extremes the intersections between real, myth and cultural reference points, as well as the way in which individual and society connect. He would pursue these relations and reference points on many occasions, but never in this way, that so aggressively went against his presumed musical or cultural background. His choice of location and character were purposeful – a place different to actual Britain, a series of significations of, in and around New York that were not just different in content but also in form and functioning from those he had been deploying up until then. The journalist Ron Ross encapsulated this extremely well, in the course of interviewing Gabriel in 1975, when he noted that 'though *The Lamb* is in many ways as idiomatically American a work as *Selling England* was British, these references [to American culture] are not meant to be token allusions to rock and roll history or pop culture', instead they were trying to simulate an immersion in that pop culture.[14] The critic Kevin Holm-Hudson, author of a book-length study of *Lamb*, added, with the benefit of hindsight, that this would have thrown the British fans of Genesis as much as American audiences would have been confused by references on *Selling England by the Pound*.[15]

The New York of *Lamb* stands in for many markers of contemporary capitalist culture – a world of shining entertainments, conformism, striving for career success, genuine creativity in the buildings and layout of the city, the movement of its people and culture. It is a city that, far from being caricatured in *Lamb*, is having its caricatures laid out side by side and twisted together like so many strands of liquorice. The underworld of most of the adventure is one guarded, defined and controlled by monsters and the fatal deadening of commerce and bureaucracy. For all that the mangled mythic city of *Lamb* lies mostly underground, it is an underworld that permeates the visible, quotidian world people tend to simply inhabit. The journey undertaken by Rael and his putatively existing brother John is framed by leaving and returning to the streets of New York, so it is at the beginning and end that we hear the more direct references to the city. From the opening track's eponymous street, the aboveground city is made strange, with Times Square becoming 'Time Square' in 'Fly on the Windshield'; masses of North American characters in 'Broadway Melody of 1974', including Canadian interloper Marshall McLuhan; and the surrealistic critique of racism in the reference to the Ku Klux Klan preparing food associated with black American culture. Holm-Hudson calls this a 'topsy-turvy universe', as everyone is set in opposition to their more expected behaviours.[16]

The key character's name tells us about the precarious status of reality with its slight juxtaposition of 'real' to 'rael', a move

that The Who had already tested as a name in their song 'Rael', in
1967. The name Rael (in *Lamb*) is about an uncertain boundary not
just between real and myth or fiction in the story of the album,
but also beyond, in the wider context of the historical world outside. The choice of his background seems unusual, indeed also a
bit forced, but let's be clear, Gabriel was not trying to convey the
reality of the existence of a real person, or even a set of cultural
signifiers as they function above ground. Rael could have any
background once he is under the streets, or when he returns,
as he 'is slotless': 'his name is supposed to be raceless', specified
Gabriel in an interview in January 1975.[17] So his background as a
Puerto Rican gang member must have been designed to do some
other work: possibly this was the beginning of Gabriel's interest
in cultures different to his own, and the growing sense of multiple
actual realities and potentials beyond those at hand in decaying
Albion. 'Americans didn't mind that I was telling them about an
American. I didn't pretend to be anything other than an observer
there for short periods. I wasn't unleashing the secrets of New
York,' Gabriel clarified, in another interview two months later.[18]
Jean Baudrillard's cultural tourism in his *America* (written in 1986)
is a useful parallel that helps to understand Gabriel's subject
position as writer of *Lamb*; both try to get inside some sort of
American reality that they are aware they cannot quite grasp.
At the same time, this leads both into somewhat problematic
positions.[19]

Alternatively, we might imagine that Gabriel had just picked a
random marginal constituency and doodled a character that was
principally revealing of his own origins as a white middle-class
man touristing in identities of which he knew very little. Or,
again, maybe the choice was more interesting still than such
caricatural readings of a caricature. Maybe Gabriel had chosen
very wisely – Rael's community was elective yet continually under
threat, both part of New York's substrate and always other, like

Puerto Rico's relation to the USA.[20] The gang membership was neither an excited embrace of criminality nor a lazy stereotype, but a sign of group belonging that was already developing in parallel to the world of upright New York. It was also part of a long list of references in *Lamb* to American popular culture, in this case the musical *West Side Story*, and also a surprisingly conscious usage of ethnicity as a given and an explicit statement of identity within New York. So it would seem that a critic of Gabriel's use (and it is a use) of 'Puerto Rican gang member' would need to be very careful of projecting their own exoticism or even a racial typing onto the presence of this character in the story of *Lamb*.

Rael also signified a more contemporary and timebound phenomenon, through the use of graffiti and tagging as not only markers of identity but ways of intervening in the fabric of New York. When we first encounter Rael in the opening, title track, he is emerging from the subway, an aerosol in hand, in charge of the city. Through tagging, the subway's potential for social mobility and the transmission of subcultures takes physical, obtrusive form, so in fact the extent of Rael's criminality, as encountered in the twists and turns of *Lamb*, is to be a pioneer in this signifying world.

Late in the album, 'The Light Dies Down on Broadway' (with lyrics by Banks and Rutherford) sees Rael emerging back to the streets, his 'home'.[21] This 'home', though, has undergone an extravagant change while Rael was away, pursued and enticed alternately by various figures of the underworld, and he emerges into a rocky ravine, clearly in some other frame of reference. This is because the New York of *Lamb* not only distorts space, it contorts time, and from as early as 'Broadway Melody' (track 3 of 24), this New York is one where all of history and prehistory is present at once, with a reference to the Everglades of Broadway – hinting both at concrete and glass growths but also to a prehistoric past that exists concurrently with 1970s Manhattan.

Peter Gabriel performing live onstage as 'Rael', the central character of *The Lamb Lies Down On Broadway*, during his last tour with Genesis, between November 1975 and May 1975.

The city is schematic but complex, a sketch that is full of detail, and home to a multilayering of constructions, growths and dimensions. It has caves, rivers, mountains, forests, hidden cities, and it is also on occasion a living beast. 'Back in N.Y.C.' renders the city of beauty and danger in one central image of the innocent urban explorer at risk of assault, bringing the real nature of the actual city into proximity. The more perversely topological the city in *Lamb*, the more it opens the question of segregation by class, race, wealth or subculture. The crossing of over- and underground takes the raw state of the city at the time and transmutes it into a machine capable of standing back from New York as mere filmic signifier. The album does not mention the crime rate of the time – after all it is a fantasy – but the real 1970s city is there, pushing at the album's apparent separation from reality and present like a threat. The city was extremely poor – or more to the point, extremely divided in wealth terms. Joshua Shannon, writing about the context for New York visual artists, summarizes this situation, and also draws out for us the similarity between Albion's modernization and change in New York:

> At the heart of the change was the fact that the city was rapidly losing its industrial base . . . The city's financial sector, meanwhile, was booming, breaking ground on countless International Style office towers. At the same time, New York's great period of urban renewal was under way, with the city's master planner, Robert Moses, seizing whole neighbourhoods for the largest 'slum clearance' program in the nation.[22]

Many were leaving the city in search of other opportunities or to avoid the relentless rise of crime. In the early 1970s, crime in New York was growing exponentially, with around 2,000 murders a year.[23] Much of Manhattan was derelict or outside legal or police control, lawless or 'down by law'. With the violence on one side and the vision of the rebirth of the financial sector of town (the fight for life, the fight to the death, of 'The Carpet Crawlers') on the other, the centre of the city – possibly Central Park – stands in for the abandonment of the urban space by any possible communal impulse. 'The Carpet Crawlers' shows us a mass of people shuffling on their knees along a heavily carpeted floor, towards an imagined ideal world. They do not question the struggle, the reason for it or why they do it, they just obey what they have been led to believe is a natural impulse. In Gabriel's *Lamb*, the activity of trying to succeed in competitive capitalism is in fact an impulse, as the drives that are taken as normal above ground are transmuted into physical, instinctive realities that allow even greater control and exploitation. Central Park's danger is conveyed in 'Back in N.Y.C.', an aggressive tune with shouted vocals by Gabriel, including a refrain about a fluffy heart in a state of waiting for rape. Given the way the city's multidimensional nature is developed and alluded to throughout *Lamb*, it would make sense to think of this as referring to the city – and the least unfluffy part would be the massive park that lies at its physical heart.

Broadway itself is more than a signifier of a particular kind of popular culture. It is one of the longitudinal avenues that define the structure of the city – there are eleven such (with a vestigial twelfth, part of the road that is the highway along the Hudson, between 22nd and 72nd streets, bordering Manhattan to the west). This is as many as there are erogenous zones in 'Counting Out Time'. That song, then, cannot be restricted to its surface-level meaning of a male narrator imagining a developing physical relation with a woman as mapped out in charts. The mapping, the charts, the precise correlation of numbers tells us that the subtext is New York as a desiring city, and one that can fulfil desire. All it takes, in *Lamb*, is a journey into a convoluted netherworld.

Broadway goes against the lateral, numbered streets; it is the most wayward street, historically preceding the grid layout, and is not only not straight, but dares to cross others, a permanent transgression of the grid.[24] The street traverses many neighbour-hoods, all strongly delineated by wealth and status but all joined transversally, at least. There is, however, no critique of wealth as such on *Lamb*, but there are numerous references to the effects of a society driven by the production of wealth, class differentiation and production, revealing the 'natural' behaviour of business to be the socially permitted extraction of labour and life – from 'The Carpet Crawlers', through 'The Grand Parade of Lifeless Packaging', to the physically distorted slippermen of the final part of the journey ('The Colony of Slippermen'). The slippermen that Rael encounters as his journey reaches the most dangerous part, where he looks for a way out, are those who have tried to cross the divide from labouring unit to wealth extractor, and their physical form reveals the album's judgements on exploitative behaviours.

The story of *Lamb* unfolds in the context of a city folding in on itself, and Gabriel's voice covers a wide range of vocal expres-sion, from whispering to shouting, via more throatily voiced parts. His voice is a lot less on edge than in the climactic parts of preceding albums, tapping into the more directed emotion of the soul singing that had inspired him in the mid-1960s. That said, there was little in the music as such that was designed to suggest anything very American, beyond the citation of 'On Broadway' in the opening, title track (perhaps because much of the music was written before Gabriel's lyrics). Instead the band developed atmospheres and provided a narrative drive to match the passage of the lyrics through various locations, scenes and encounters. The atmosphere conjured up by the music is at its least interesting in the instrumental tracks, where the 'jamming' that the four musicians of the band enjoyed so much is given free rein, and when their attempt to 'be atmospheric' is too transparent; but the

fierce music of 'Back in N. Y. C.', is closer to Suicide's first album
of pulsing electro-punk (released in 1977) than to composer and
folklorist Vaughan Williams's Albion, and the pulsating climaxes
at various points in the album, coming more regularly as the
album progresses ('The Waiting Room', 'Colony of Slippermen',
'Riding the Scree', 'it'), offer the outlines of a properly formal and
complete work.

The presence of American music in English progressive rock,
however, was much greater than was usually presumed, with
progressive rock often misleadingly characterized as a product
of church and classical music. In fact, it primarily developed out
of American jazz, folk revival and expansion of the rock form.
The first concept albums were American (Duke Ellington, Frank
Sinatra), and the exploration of widening the instrumentation
of popular music took place in America as much as in Britain or
mainland Europe. The (Broadway) musical was, and still is, an
underestimated source for the expansion of concert performance
as a multimedia musical work, as well as offering inspiration
for thematic unity, repeated refrains and excursions on themes
present in musicals. In this sense, *West Side Story* (1957, music by
Leonard Bernstein, libretto by Stephen Sondheim) was more present in *Lamb's* Manhattan than might initially seem the case, with
Rael a survivor of the musicalized gang fight, transported into
and across multiple realities of the city.

Other progressive bands had tapped the musical directly, with
The Nice performing a radicalized version of 'America' in 1968,
releasing it as a single; Yes had covered Paul Simon's 'America'
and included segments of the Bernstein/Sondheim piece (they
also covered 'Something's Coming' from *West Side Story*, with this
appearing on the B-side of 'Sweetness' in 1969). Genesis delved
deeper and more strangely into American culture, and sought to
replicate the working of a musical, with songs of very different
structures, lyrical intent and mood, diverging widely from pop

songs or even the then lengthening progressive epics, while still continuing to push in a coherent narrative direction. They were to some extent still caught up in the outsider's perception of Broadway as representing something essential about America.[25] In the complex, arguably convoluted, structure and lyrics at the core of *Lamb*, American culture was shown in a more advanced light, with Gabriel consciously adopting the position of outsider, all the while identifying competing and even cascading othernesses within American culture, as exemplified in the topography of New York and Rael's unwitting quest through its hidden functionalities of business, finance and drive to prioritize conformism over rebellious creativity.

The presentation of *Lamb* in concert was completed, as was now customary on Genesis tours, by a highly dynamic and character-based performance from Gabriel himself, mostly as Rael, and towards the end in serpentine white bodysuit for 'The Lamia', where Rael encounters three snake-like female creatures that act as sexual sirens but who are poisoned by Rael's blood when they attempt to devour him. Rael is lured in, but cannot be ingested by the city, by the consuming desires that guard the ways in and out. There are psychological subtexts, too, but it is Jung rather than Freud whom Gabriel cited as a reference, one that was 'deliberate to some extent'; but much more significant was his stress on Rael as 'an outcast in a totally alien situation'.[26] Following 'The Lamia', Gabriel would don the bulbous buboes of the slippermen costume ('The Colony of Slippermen'), which illustrated the corruption of the souls of those caught up trying to succeed in a commercially driven and prison-like society, as their transformation is made flesh. Collins has mentioned this costume as one of the most problematic parts of the staging, musing that Gabriel had not really thought through the practicalities.[27]

Gabriel's costume interventions had previously represented a range of roles and ideas, with him saying in 1973 that 'my part has been to conceive all the characters and masks I can from a piece' and going on to imagine a future merging of media – the realization of which came in the multimedia *Lamb* tour.[28] In another interview, in 1974, he spoke of preparations for the staging of *Lamb*, hopeful of 'a panoramic scene, [that] will relate closer to what we're doing on stage than the family snapshsots we tried last time'.[29]

This tour, his last with Genesis, saw a greatly simplified look in terms of costume at least. Replacing fox head and red dress, or head flower, was the leather jacket and jeans of the central gang member, emphasizing not a reduction but an extension of the music, with performance there to enhance the music: 'I think showmanship is justifiable,' said Gabriel, 'if it adds drama and doesn't swamp the music.'[30] Even Gabriel's short hair stood out against a backdrop of the dominant long-haired look for rock and most pop stars of the 1970s. Somewhat problematically for today's audiences perhaps, Gabriel had also applied make-up to darken his complexion. To pre-empt potential critics of cultural appropriation who might point to a white man taking on the mask of 'other' cultures through this heightened visibility, Gabriel's face was in fact coloured a mix of red, brown and silver, with huge blocks of blue-black colour around eyelid and brow. In other words, it was transparently visible that Gabriel's Rael face was not of this world, but one that was a sign of an excessive play-acting, rather than a misguided attempt to pass in any way as a specific, earthly, other.

Beyond the character of Rael, and behind the band, over a thousand images played on multiple slide carousels in a triptych projection (the slide show was devised by Gabriel and developed by Jeffrey Shaw, with Theo Botschuijver), offering images from the album's lyrics and song titles, as well as expanding on them visually. The opening section of *Lamb* was mirrored by many images of New York, and further on there was a mixed use of collage, illustration, photographs staged and found, existing artworks (notably by surrealist painters), and numerous images of the Manhattan cityscape and its inhabitants.

For the most part, the images illustrated individual lyrical images or ideas, rather than developing the narrative or revealing further layers. The shots of New York covered the gamut of popular entertainment images, realist portrayals of lower-income areas and people, and the range of activities across the span of a day in the city, like a condensed (and less detailed) version of Chantal Akerman's experimental film *Letters from Home* (1977). That film concentrated on creating a visual portrait of the city in long shots that remade the city as a strange set of repetitive or banal gestures and movements. Akerman's voiceover was her reading letters sent to her from her mother while the director lived in New York between 1971 and 1973. The overall effect was one of a contortion of space and time, very similar to that achieved by Gabriel and Genesis in *Lamb*.

The visuals and dramatic performance by Gabriel amounted to a far more complex proposition than that on offer by other progressive bands, several of which were playing to extremely large audiences in the u.s. by 1974. David Bowie's character sketches on

Slide show from *The Lamb Lies Down on Broadway*, projected behind Genesis onstage.

which shows were hung were also considerably less developed than the multimedia work within which Gabriel, as Rael, prowled: 'the characters I [Gabriel] play are things talked about in the lyrics, and they do occur. Bowie's a great writer, but I don't always think his costumes are relevant to the music.'[31] As well as the great inventiveness of Gabriel, there is a more down-to-earth explanation for this advance on all others: it was phenomenally difficult to stage multimedia performances in an era before computer automation and sequencing / synchronization. The visuals must certainly have helped carry the show (despite Collins's misgivings), which offered the very demanding proposition of listening to a new double album in its entirety.

While American audiences worked hard at these concerts, as they had to process an as yet unheard album in full, and the u.s. profile of Genesis was being raised, Gabriel was intent on leaving, informing the band late in 1974. He agreed to complete the European *Lamb* tour, with the plan of exiting in 1975. He finally departed in mid-1975, announcing the news publicly in July of that year. He launched his solo career two years later, in a concert in New Jersey on 5 March 1977, already cutting the amount of Genesis material to almost nothing (the only Genesis song was 'Back in n.y.c.'). He played in New York state on the second night of the tour and was in New York City as a solo artist by 19 March.[32] On this tour he revisited his soul interest with two Marvin Gaye songs: 'Ain't That Peculiar', on the setlist of the North American tour, and 'I Heard It Through the Grapevine' on the European follow-up leg.

The band that had assembled in Toronto for the recording of what would be the first *Peter Gabriel* was nearly all of American provenance, with producer Bob Ezrin from Canada and Robert Fripp from the recently rested avant-garde progressive band King Crimson the exceptions (though Fripp was resident in New York at the time). So we have plenty of circumstantial evidence of a role for New York and the U.S. in Gabriel's nascent solo career, but it was perhaps the variety of musical genres that had been covered by his new band members that really drove his new approach – as they came from rock, jazz, disco, soul and funk backgrounds, often having played across genres themselves. For Gabriel, this clearly represented an opening up to non-English music, an opening up from what he saw as a now generic music, for all that progressive rock's roots were eclectic in the extreme. It is through musical opening up that Gabriel would play out his games of self-identity on his first four solo albums.

Peter Gabriel in Central Park, New York, 1977.

3 PETER GABRIEL, PETER GABRIEL, PETER GABRIEL, PETER GABRIEL

With the first *Peter Gabriel* album, Gabriel set out on a sequence of four albums with that name (or without title, but *with* that name). To avoid confusion, people have titled them 1, 2, 3 and 4, as confirmed in the prominent placing of PGCD1, PGCD2, PGCD3 and PGCD4 on the spines of the first generation release of the albums on CD. Fans have also adopted 'Car', 'Scratch', 'Melt' and 'Security' respectively as alternative titles, based on the cover images. Renaming the albums seems to miss a very important point: either Gabriel was giving up on titles altogether, or he was asserting his position as creator of these four releases (probably a bit of both). In either case – that is, in both – he is playing with his identity as a rock star, challenging marketing strategies, making them part of a non-moving sequence, making them part of a self-expression we can easily presume to have been progressively stifled in the context of Genesis.

The four albums marked out an ever more rigorous terrain of musical experimentation and play, going from the somewhat dated eclecticism of 1977's *Peter Gabriel*, through the sharper, new wave minimalism of *Peter Gabriel* (1978), into the embrace of musics beyond Western genres that arrived on *Peter Gabriel* (1980) and flowed free on 1982's *Peter Gabriel*. The role of percussion changed dramatically, the songwriting became stranger, the thematic and formal focus growing with each release. In tandem with the musical changes, Gabriel explored multiple modes of being across the albums, often focusing on marginal figures on the edge, or moving through the hinterlands of contemporary living – and these situations are what will be explored below as the essence of the lyrics and ideas on all four records. Gabriel also expanded his use of media, notably in the form of music video – in 1978 he was already 'involved in a video-disc project'[1] – and began to work through permutations of concert staging that were both a riposte to progressive rock and a further move in developing his own methods of embodying theme and character, in ways that are properly musically and artistically progressive. While not very achievable at the time, Gabriel was highly enthused by the prospect of hi-tech audiovisual futures, developing ideas with the journalist and theorist Stewart Kranz. These ideas ranged from holograms of performers, to various surround sound and visual systems, to more interactive, games-based art products that listeners could work on, direct and make evolve. This collaboration of ideas took place in 1978–9 and was outlined by Gabriel and Kranz in an interview in early 1979. Gabriel summed up their speculative mission as finding

> Some ways that will ultimately help new artists reach more people at less expense. That's the kind of technological progress we'd like to see. Plus anything that grants the audience more opportunity to interact with the artist.[2]

By 1977, the progressive rock genre was arguably in poor shape, suffering the onslaught of punk but also caught up in self-induced fatigue and (formal) decadence, typified in stadium rock and ever more intricate presentations of music. That is, of course, one way of looking at it; another would be to note that post-punk, post-disco, the main progressive rock bands were *more* successful, not less. Punk had induced a sort of 'year zero' approach to music, and the past was to be swept away without a process of triage as to what could have been worth saving. Punk aimed to be simple and aggressive not for the sake of it, but to represent an alienation both social and aesthetic. In the case of the former, Western industrial societies were teetering on the edge of economic collapse. But where punk decried 'no future' for citizens, it decreed 'no past' for music, in a bid to reconnect to the audience and overcome the (supposed) alienation felt by them. Progressive rock was complex, was something that its audiences probably could not play – that, after all, was part of the fascination. But the technical and creative innovation of massive stretching of the rock form meant that the rush of shared creation was being lost, at least from the point of view of pro-punk journalism (and there was a parallel in the micro-scenes of free improvised music around Europe at exactly the same time).

But we underestimate progressive rock's capacity for variation if we look only at the iceberg tip of its excess and ignore the experimentation that continued apace in the late 1970s, in music often labelled as 'art rock' or avant-garde. Gabriel, like his sparring partner Robert Fripp (lead guitarist in pioneering progressive band King Crimson), took the view that anything labelled progressive had become at best misguided, at worst cynical and foolish. So, ironically, they both went on to make music that is progressive music at its best, as opposed to replicating styles and structures that had become generic. Gabriel emerged from the critical wreckage (in the UK at least) to slot in alongside gloomy synth pop, new wave and post-punk art rock such as that purveyed by Magazine and Wire. These two bands epitomized post-punk music that maintained the energy and critique of punk, but without shedding an interest in complex lyrical ideas and formal and musical innovation. The use of electronics in a wide range of popular music and the minimizing of blatant instrumental 'prowess' were things to which Gabriel's growing public could align his music. In the U.S., these genres were largely shorthanded as 'new wave', and few would have categorized Peter Gabriel's early solo albums as partaking of the progressive rock mode. But it is more accurate to say that experimental pop music had changed tack, and now new, yet still song-based, genres were arising, crossovers abetted by the early shoots of globalization. Gabriel soon became one of the drivers of this change.

But that is not how Gabriel's solo album career started out. The first album brought together a set of largely American musicians, two of whom, Larry Fast and Tony Levin, would become mainstays of his bands over subsequent years. The music made some reference to more American parts of rock history, but above all, this album was part of the mainstream pomp rock or progressive pop of the decade – Elton John, 10cc, Supertramp – though with an American twist worthy of a more epic Billy Joel. There was a lot of piano, some misguided blues ('Waiting for the Big One', which even featured Gabriel attempting a kind of grizzled, random American accent from some unidentifiable part of the u.s.), and disco rock in 'Down the Dolce Vita'. The album was very consciously 'more a bunch of songs', as Gabriel described it, in order to move away from high concept and formal complexity.[3]

The album was the beginning of Gabriel's exploration of characters who occupy contemporary society, today's world, without being able to dwell in it, such as the melancholy of 'Moribund the Burgermeister''s need to police the city, or the narrator of 'Modern Love', who fantasizes his way around the world of great artworks with a surreptitious and barely contained eroticism. There is also a hint of global disaster ahead – the earthquake that will be the 'big one', or the deluge of 'Here Comes the Flood', both flickers of an oneiric or imagined apocalypse ahead. The latter song carries considerably much more charge when reprised on Fripp's *Exposure* (1979), where its bombastic chorus music is stripped away entirely, replaced by an insistent soundscape from

Advertisement for the first *Peter Gabriel* album.

Fripp, and preceded by the mystic J. G. Bennett musing on the flooding of the planet.

When it comes to location and signification, though, one song stands out – Gabriel's first solo hit, 'Solsbury Hill'. The name refers to a real hill in Somerset, site of an ancient hill fort. Where 'Here Comes the Flood' contrasts an exploration of the power of nature with industrial living, 'Solsbury Hill' is named but not explored. Instead it comes to stand in for a rebirth of Gabriel's creativity in the freedom of not being 'part of the machinery', as the lyrics have it. The rural location and numerous thinly disguised references seem to indicate it was about the leaving of Genesis, about abandoning something that has got caught up in commercial pressures, and how Gabriel himself felt the mounting pressure of being ready to leave but agreeing to stay, as 'part of the scenery'. It was not sniping at his bandmates, label or public, but standing back to look at the overall, total absurdity of his Genesis life as he saw it. More recently (2011), he has said of it that 'when I left Genesis, I just wanted to be out of the music business. I felt like I was just in the machinery. We knew what we were going to be doing in 18 months or two years ahead. I just did not enjoy that.'[4]

The rural epiphany is unexpected, after the ultra-urban complexity of *The Lamb Lies Down on Broadway*, but is evidence that he was escaping himself as located in Genesis, as much as leaving the others. So as a process of psychological self-locating, 'Solsbury Hill' was both highly personal and a comment on a world dominated by notions of the importance of wealth, possessions, fame, being part of an urban facelessness, and believing it to be the right or the good way to live. On all the *Peter Gabriel* albums, people push against being caught in normativity, in bowing to subtly exploitative expectations of success.

'Solsbury Hill' was Gabriel identifying the importance of getting out of the humdrum and into what seems a simpler way of living.[5] But the hill was only a guiding vision, not the endpoint. For all his consciousness of nature, Gabriel was interested in heightening our awareness, not insisting on a dogma of 'back to nature'. So the song was about being able to separate ideology from reality, with an almost Marxist sense of how workers, consumers, commuters got fooled into believing in the quest for the baubles of exchange value. Gabriel would never overtly subscribe to an ideology, even a critical one, stating in 1978 that 'I don't have faith in large organisations, in large groups or the ideologies which are supposed to appeal to them.'[6] While he would soon become involved in politics, he has maintained this position throughout his career, regarding groups that work for rights, to end poverty, to prevent violence, as all being non-ideological, not subject to dogma. Within the allusive political critique of 'Solsbury Hill' is something else, though, and that is the notion of 'home': the chorus, such as it is (one line marking the end of almost unchanging thematic repetition in the music), is all about being brought or guided home, and in the final iteration of the refrain, he sloughs off material concerns to accompany those who would bring him home: '"Hey", I said, "You can keep my things / they've come to take me home."'

The simple music, an always returning riff, and the chorus, returning to the idea of 'home' itself, all point to the kind of mystification (the misty-eyed and false impression) of the rural that Raymond Williams complained about and that, as I argued earlier, Gabriel's lyrics in Genesis had mostly superceded – so what was the 'home' here? Instead of a reversion to traditional modes of viewing rural Albion as ever-present, merely awaiting unveiling, the 'home' of 'Solsbury Hill' was not there until discovered in the song; it comes into being as 'home' retrospectively, *as if it were already home* and as if Gabriel were now home, even though he is there for the first time. The home was a way out: of Genesis, of a rock rat race, maybe away from someone he had become (summarized in 'the machinery' line, symbolizing industrial alienation as well as biographical discontent). Home arrived as a location of willed and desired loss. This is not a gratuitous speculation – it will in fact be confirmed on many occasions in the twenty-first century when Gabriel has made literal the idea of home as being a return, in his various revisitations and rethinkings of his oeuvre, in as direct a musical form as the listener/speculator thinking about 'home' in 'Solsbury Hill' could wish for. This is without even thinking about the triumphant air-punching cries of 'home' in live performances of the song as a return to the stadium rock it wanted to leave behind.

The first solo album was geographically unfocused compared to the later albums he had made with Genesis, in addition to being made up of too great a variety of stylistic and musical elements to add up to a satisfying whole. The *Peter Gabriel* of 1977 was adrift, not yet the sure-footed traveller of later *Peter Gabriels*, but already open-eyed about subjectivity and creativity as being necessarily on the move.

In *Peter Gabriel* (1978), the stories, characters and settings flit from one borderland to another. Gabriel referred, in interview, to the ways in which he tried to express his own hidden selves and those of others, and in so doing, capture an image of society: 'we're all composed of many people,' he said, and he was 'us[ing] images to communicate feelings rather than change the way the world is going', while acknowledging the 'consciousness of what goes on in day-to-day life'.[7] To get at that complex picture and make it suggestively critical entailed exploring unfamiliar or borderline states. Sometimes entrapped, sometimes free and outside the law, at other times lost in zones beyond society, a sequence of narrators expresses transient living conditions in fixed locations or dogged fixity in transitional locations and spaces. This is an album about 'borderline cases', a term that appears explicitly in the fifth track, 'White Shadow', but helps clarify the ambience or intent of the album as a whole. These cases pertain to mentalities, or other ways in which people's position in society is marginal. These situations create dislocations, with the different ways of living on borderlines coalescing. While most of Gabriel's albums do have a thematic unity, or at least an identifiable set of points of interest, along with a cohesive musical statement, I would have to say that the first two *Peter Gabriel* albums do not seem to have this centring. But the second one begins to show us how he will centre his solo album releases, and that is through sets of themes, ideas and explorations of psychological conditions that connect, but without forming a single narrative thread.

This 1978 *Peter Gabriel* offered a clear, if initially amorphous, set of connections between individual states of mind and spaces at the margins. To summarize the ways space coheres the songs, a list of the kind of spaces on offer in the lyrics can lead us on to the correct path, and these are: the air, a shed, the street, (leaving) a shop, some sort of desert wilderness, (leaving) home, (leaving) home (to join the army), the open, washed up (somewhere), the world (Gaia), home (where a murder occurs), and home (acquired from proceeds of that murder). Characters move through spaces but find it hard to dwell in them; they commit crimes, reflect on violence and keep moving, restless in the twilight or streetlight, away from the view of the others. When contact is made, it is mostly in the form of a suppressed conflict or the expression of oppositional outsiderness. Whereas Gabriel would soon begin a long career marked by political awareness, engagement and action, and change his ideas of being and belonging accordingly (as of *Peter Gabriel*, 1980, but hinted at here), what was presented were ungrounded individuals, separated off from any sense of community, in a way that represented both an exclusion and an assertion of autonomy, beyond societal norms. Gabriel became aware at this point that 'the political', in the broadest sense of engagement, was something possible for an artist without making their music into a vehicle for dogma. He singled out for praise Tom Robinson, whose 'Glad to Be Gay' (released in February 1978) was part of the singer's prominent gay rights and left-wing activism, for his engaged rock music and for his proposing a way for subtle political or social comment to work in song:

> I think that quite often songs that are just political have a blandness which doesn't appeal to me, yet, equally, songs which have no consciousness of what goes on in day-to-day life have the same effect. I suppose my music's prime purpose is to use images to communicate feelings rather than change the way the world is going.[8]

The vast majority of individual or social character development on the album occured at the lyrical level, but there was also a vast range of character-defining vocals – with Gabriel explicitly developing a character through vocal style, such as the rasping shout of Mozo, a step beyond Rael in *The Lamb Lies Down on Broadway*. Mozo was a character that was never fully fledged, but ghosted through a few early Gabriel songs. In the opening track of *Peter Gabriel* (1978), 'On the Air', he declares his presence on the airwaves and also in the city, being helpful but invisible: 'I want everyone to know that Mozo is here.' Mozo is like air, but also stands as a presence that audio technology can effectively create through radio wave dissemination. This mysterious character gives way in the second track, 'D.I.Y.', to an assertive individual, maybe a loner, who praises the independent spirit of 'just doing it yourself', the craft of making things, and also the capitalist ethos that was the attenuated remnant of ideas of self-improvement. Where 'do it yourself' had previously signified a pioneer or Protestant work ethic, it was now something about home or bodily improvement fads (the latter tracked out on record from Lyn Marshall's yoga to Jane Fonda's workouts as the 1970s moved into the more assertive and image-oriented self-reliance of the 1980s).

Those two tracks matched lyrics with music, the band latching on to and propulsing Gabriel's vocal anger, and they cleared a space for the more complicated interactions of voice and instrumentation later. Where the previous year's *Peter Gabriel* had too often been smothered in pacifying orchestration, this album was more coherent and simple, 'more spontaneous', precision replacing the display of skill.[9] Gabriel observed in 2016 that his producer Robert Fripp was highly influential in this regard: 'He was very keen to try speeding up my recording process, as many people have been since and failed, but he got closest to it.'[10] Fripp admits that he moved from minor participant on the first *Peter Gabriel* to being a strong, driving component on the second *Peter Gabriel*, saying in late 1978 that 'my creative part was much more important on the second album. In fact, the difference between these two albums is Fripp.'[11]

The album was at its most interesting when the musical part contrasted strongly with the lyrics and vocal delivery, and this was most striking on two tracks that break down the idea of home. In 'Indigo', the narrator has to leave – and is currently living an alienated, isolated life, despite seeming to live with his family. We are not told why he is leaving, only that he is. The music, though, conveys little of the drama that the words hint at: a past, elsewhere, that means that 'here' is only relative, a late discovery of safety, now to be lost. 'Home Sweet Home', the song that closes the album, is even darker, echoing a strategy developed by Serge Gainsbourg in the early 1970s, where music would explicitly create not just a contrasting atmosphere to the lyrics, but one designed to lull the listener, masking the import of what they were in some way consenting to, accepting the song they were hearing, without considering the lyrics.

The home of this particular song is the site of a double suicide of the narrator's wife and daughter, conveyed as if it could have been a double murder, that is, with some responsibility on the part of the one telling the story. The family had been living on the eleventh storey of a tower block, bringing us back to the trauma of Britain's cheap modernism that Gabriel had explored with Genesis and making it directly lethal. The insurance payout allows the narrator to gamble money; he wins, and buys a big traditional house in the countryside (another Genesis return, this time to perverse rural Albion). All the while, Gabriel sings gently, not even with melancholy, but with a sort of distant puzzlement and acceptance, which by the end has become an abstention from responsibility. A gentle, steady tune acts as the backdrop, with 'emotive' saxophone near the end, which is just as likely to be about pleasure as sorrow. By the late 1970s, the instrument had come to signify ready emotion in pop music, via fusion, album-oriented rock, as well as blues, soul or jazz – a bland transplantation of a particular set of instrumental strategies into another terrain, that of pop or rock, and part of the defining smoothness of 'adult contemporary' (invented in 1979 as a rebranding of the U.S. 'easy listening' chart). The vocal delivery of the track heightens the lyrical intent, pushing the idea that 'home' is the privileged site of alienation through its wilfully misleading way of signifying the lyrical content.

The spaces in this second album were not all abstract – the would-be army recruit of 'Animal Magic' is destined for Northern Ireland, site of a conflict over national belonging and ownership. The long-running period known as The Troubles was at its peak at this point, with many killed on both sides over the fight for Irish national sovereignty, in ambush, by bombs, informers, and often by accident. To be clear, Gabriel did not have anything to say on that conflict, but was aware of its presence in British and Irish life at the time as a marker of hidden danger and violence. It is the reflection on how space and being interact that was the dominant political and/or social comment here, insofar as there was one. The track 'Exposure' gave a clue as to the importance of spatialization, of rethinking locatedness from a personal or social point of view (hence there is also a track entitled 'Perspective'). 'Exposure' is simple, repetitive, insistent, cold funk emptiness. Other than the repeated word 'exposure', Gabriel sings that the 'I' of the song wants to be in the open: 'space is what I need.' Space and openness generally suggest a consensual, willed presence in a particular area or terrain, but the word exposure carries a very different set of suggestions: surveillance, fear, being forced to be out in the open, and for Gabriel this was part of understanding himself as located in an alienated society, saying to Penny Valentine, of his second album, that he was 'trying to communicate feelings and ideas that also express what I feel about society'.[12] Exposure suggests nothing like freedom, but the use of open space to police activity. At the same time, it can also be about self-exposure – both revealing your innermost being in public, and flashing your genitals. In very few words, and in the claustrophobia of repetition, I think Gabriel and his co-writer Fripp managed to capture all of those, thereby grasping and working with a very complex idea of social space.

Once we add these different approaches to location to the range of identified places and settings in this *Peter Gabriel*, it becomes clear that Gabriel was working through a rethinking of the notion of space, of location, such that these were not about specific places or even reactions to them – they have no reality outside being experienced. Spaces have no fixed way of being defined – they can be an identified place, like a city, or they can be more abstract, like nature, or the wild, but that is not the end of it. Space is brought into being in different ways – so some of the songs are about being in certain places, and others about how that happens; others still are about places as something from which to be distant or separate. In addition to this phenomenological complexity, where it is the interaction between subject and object that rings both into being, so that each makes the other real, listeners are obliged to take heed of the importance of specifically marginal spaces – either temporally, because being passed through, or physically, because oddly located, or socially, because unacceptably occupied or used.

These kinds of marginal spaces were identified by the artist, experimental architect and urbanist Gordon Matta-Clark in his *Reality Properties: Fake Estates* (1973). In that work, Matta-Clark bought up small pieces of land that lay unclaimed between lands covered by individual property deeds in New York (mostly in Queens, one in Staten Island), making a new property that could never form an integrated whole and that existed only due to the accidentally interstitial nature of legal property contracts. This is exactly the kind of thinking that can be heard on *Peter Gabriel* (1978) and that would be developed on *Peter Gabriel* in 1980. Matta-Clark was not only uncovering a peculiar real-world surrealism, he was also revealing the arbitrariness of the institution of property, and so his was political work. Gabriel's songs were gradually recovering the sort of tangential politics of his later Genesis years, and when these blossomed on the subsequent album, ideas of individual and social being moved to the core of his thinking and found solid musical parallels, so that the music became a carrier of meaning as opposed to being the 'backing'. This began on more expansive tracks such as 'White Shadow' and in the defamiliarization strategy of contrasting music with lyrics, but if space on the second *Peter Gabriel* was all about an inherent transient slipperiness, then on the third *Peter Gabriel* it is about mobilizing that space, those spaces, those ways of being, and altering or twisting those spaces.

Gabriel's 1980 album was more tightly conceived, musically and lyrically, than its two predecessors. The album was in two parts, which offered contrasting focal points, with side 1 (on vinyl) consisting of a near-conceptual sequence of songs that centre on characters at the edge of civilized, policed society, and side 2 taking on broader political topics. The two halves were far from separate, linked by a new muscular, percussion-centred music with many more synthesized components. The drumming, provided by Jerry Marotta and Phil Collins, was defined by Gabriel's novel decision to remove all the clanging metal parts that habitually sit at the top of the rock drummer's equipment and that had mushroomed into a whole trebly and splashy ecosystem at the hands of progressive rock drummers. Freed, perhaps unwillingly, from many of their stock moves, particularly in using cymbal or hi-hat as punctuation, the drummer on each track set up a rolling, pulsing set of rhythms. The heaviness of this new drum set was aided by the use of 'gated reverb' effects, made more famous by Collins in the drum break of 'In the Air Tonight' a year later. In addition, there was plenty of programmed percussion (as in 'Biko'), even replacing 'real' drums on some tracks. The net effect was to create a brooding atmosphere that worked in tandem with the lyrics and relatively simple musical composition, which used its guitars very covertly. The overall drum sound was designed to take listeners away from Western set convention, but without simulating anyone else's percussion as such. The key was the removal of a familiar style, to lead the listener to unfamiliar psychologies and actions in order to question what is taken as familiar, normal, in a society turned in on itself: 'it's easier to look at things and analyse what's happening if you push it to extremes,' Gabriel said of the album.[13] When the album was re-released on vinyl in 2016, Gabriel made a point of emphasizing how he had sought out new percussion sounds on which to build these visions, bringing in 'new wave' producer Hugh Padgham, and also had attempted to incorporate minimalist, repetitive percussion to get away from easily digestible rock.[14] At the same time, similar themes were being musically realized in new wave, in post-punk, on Talking Heads's *Remain in Light* (also

Peter Gabriel (1977).

Peter Gabriel (1978).

Peter Gabriel (1980).

Peter Gabriel (1982).

:leased in 1980), in some of the darker songs by The Police, and in emergent goth music.

The first part of *Peter Gabriel* (1980) is made up of five different stories, all narrated in the first person, from singular viewpoints, way beyond what is normal. Gabriel inhabits these characters, trying to get at the thrill of sociopathy as hobby or need, and all of these characters move surreptitiously, in the dark, round the fences, but getting inside people's heads, and normal society doubles its controlling effects in response to mounting panic. The inhabitants of this album are, in the words of the journalist Dave Marsh, variations on 'an "innocent" character who watches the corruption of society from a distance until he finds himself being pulled inexorably toward the center of events'.[15] The continuity of threatening affect is disturbed by the saxophone-dominated 'Start', hived-off from 'I Don't Remember' (it remains part of that track on the record's German version, *Ein deutsches Album*), out of place in formal terms, as the others all have content that is about misplaced drives.[16] With 'Intruder', the listener accompanies the narrator into houses, exploring people's lives and possessions while they sleep; in 'No Self Control', the spectre of violence erupting from tension is uppermost; 'I Don't Remember' is not just about memory but about isolation; 'Family Snapshot' is about murdering a politician (echoing the assassination of John F. Kennedy, but actually Alabama governor George Wallace); and 'And Through the Wire' describes another separation, or isolation practice. Each of these tracks presents its own take on spatialization and subjectivity. The exploration of extreme 'states of mind' that Gabriel conveyed as being the main drive behind the third *Peter Gabriel* was something that Phil Sutcliffe pursued with the artist in interview, and, disarming and deflecting as always, Gabriel conceded that he was perhaps something of 'a purveyor of amateur psychiatric clichés'.[17]

In 'Intruder', the sanctity of one's own home, one's safe dwelling place, is disrupted. The intruder insinuates himself into your life and thrills at breaking through something like the theatre's fourth wall. The home becomes pervious, and the intruder comes and goes through his own dimensions, unhindered by what we take to be solid. The narrator of 'No Self Control' is like the dromomaniacs at the core of Paul Virilio's *Speed and Politics*, a book in which the cultural theorist proposed the idea that modernity was essentially about the bid to move ever faster and further, and could no longer prevent itself moving onward.[18] The 'need to move' of Virilio's dromomania began as an outlying, avant-garde activity but infiltrated all of modern society (and Virilio was writing this in 1977): the narrator of 'No Self Control' is walking endlessly, is perpetually on the move in order to get somewhere, but that somewhere is in fact caught up in the process of movement. Again, Gabriel identifies space as something defined through action, through perception. For this narrator, interiors develop their own threats – the domestic becomes uncanny, *unheimlich*.

'I Don't Remember' is only partially about amnesia – it is much more concerned with loss of subjectivity and recognizably, offically determined identity: 'I got no means to show identification,' declares the narrator. The 'I' of the song cannot understand what people are saying. While this does connect to the idea of the refugee, to the trauma of a suffering outsider, the delivery of the lyric, over Tony Levin's rolling bass pulse, suggests more an assumption of an absence of identity, a rejection of the puerile and dogmatic tenets of identity formation in favour of Gabriel's term 'states of mind', which he proposed with regard to the subject-matter of this album (and which could apply to all the stories and characters in his work).[19] The evidence for this is in the continual repetition of the word 'I': when all the bureaucratic, official and nationalistic contours of identity are stripped away, there is still the subject, even if he or she has been rendered

meaningless – re-grounded in himself as opposed to in a politically or linguistically defined place.

In 'Family Snapshot', the assassin is asserting his existence in
the world, moving from silent margin to becoming a hidden infil-
trator who can have an effect on and in the real spaces of the city
and attack its political representative, thereby closing the space in
on itself as rejected. For the assassin-narrator, the media reporting
will clear a domain where his presence can be known, where he is
not just a faceless, skulking non-person. The yearning of the sections that most resemble a chorus suggest the early rejection that
brought the character to this point, and Gabriel soulfully opens
this up at the end, singing directly to that one boy's rejection, to
the lack of attention in his family home. Without being overly
sympathetic to this character's actions, Gabriel tries to assess
where the motivation came from, trying to track, as he said of the
song, 'patterns of behaviour begun in childhood [that] do carry
through', and once more, the domestic interior is shown as a place
of danger, or of loss and isolation.[20]

The song sequence closes with the view from outside the
fences of paranoid middle-class living. 'And Through the Wire'
is how the poor see this separate, wilfully isolated segment of
society, and threaten to come through the wire fences at the
same time as taking over the airwaves. The city is a constructed
alienation machine, perpetuating class distinction and emptying
of interaction, other than that mediated by protective armours of
all sorts, whether physical or mental. The word 'border' returns
to suggest, again, the eventual assumption of outsiderness that
exclusion has created: you want us outside? We are the outside,
comes the assertive reply, we lie in wait at the edges of your containment – and this is what the 'we' of the song conveys, as well
as the sense that the real community is now to be found outside
– that is the place where a reactive 'we' has grown, despite the will
to drive that 'us' away.

The second part of the album begins with Gabriel's first big hit single, 'Games Without Frontiers' (giving him his first UK top ten chart placing, a feat he would not repeat until 'Sledgehammer' in 1986, a hit of yet another level of magnitude), the title and chorus of which refers to the TV game, launched in 1965, that was designed to pit teams from across Europe in jovial opposition, as opposed to fighting each other. This slapstick mirror of what was then the European Economic Community was called *Jeux Sans Frontières*, or in its UK version, *It's a Knockout*. Where the first set of tracks looks to margins and what is forced to the border, 'Games Without Frontiers' looks at the possibility of borders losing their meaning, while at the same time decrying war. It does this through its reference to the knockabout game show, and this mediatized game, far from being ridiculous here, or perhaps because of its willingness to be absurd, is posited as the model for international cooperation. The maintenance of borders is to be shunned, driven away in the spirit of continual unity, where competition and diversity persist, but not through predetermined limits and enclosures. 'Not One of Us' has a simple political message, which is about the categorization of foreigners, outsiders, as others. This is a message that has taken on more weight and significance in the course of recent years, as populist politicians court fears by demonizing groups of people in a world reshaped on globalized corporate terms.

Something curious happens in 'Not One of Us', as the border to be critiqued, undermined and subverted is the body, hence the importance of the opening line 'it's only water'. This declaimed statement refers to the tangible geographical difference that arises between islands, or between an island and a bigger land mass. It also refers to what connects – as the oceans and rivers form subsystems that pay no heed to political or ethnic barriers. Lastly, it refers to the significance attributed to blood in the *jus sanguinis* that defines the right to belong to a group of citizens through blood, that is, heredity. The notion that blood is thicker than water cuts both ways here – first, it illustrates the flimsiness of basing belonging on liquid; second, it takes the opposed view that 'it's only water' that connects us, and not blood. Gabriel's vocal makes it unclear what 'only' is doing here – whether it is performing the task of a critical undermining or just dismissive of an other's claim is kept ambiguous, and I believe this ambiguity is entirely purposeful. The sense in this song of not belonging connects us to the narratives of social and psychological alienation of the first half of the album. Anyone can become 'not one of us', as the person who is not part of the whole has no say in defining whether they belong or not. The next track, with the slow development of its theme, follows up the internal alienation focus, and its title of 'Lead a Normal Life' is tied up in the impossibility, even undesirability, of so doing, and mockingly echoes the insistence on obeying a series of arbitrary social diktats that have come to be seen as common sense.

Up to this point, this third *Peter Gabriel* developed an intertwined set of ideas about political, emotional and social division, and it did this through maintaining a coherent instrumental practice where rhythm and repetition hold sway. Every part of each track contributes to the meaning of the song – the message and the signification. With 'Biko', something shifted, as Gabriel was talking about a real person, and unlike the abstracted killer in 'Family Snapshot', this time it was a victim – but also a heroic critic – of a real, oppressive regime that gave the song its subject-matter. 'Biko' confirmed the move of the rest of the album towards a merging of personal and political, which was also to define Gabriel's very public attitude and actions through the 1980s. As with his images of New York on *Lamb*, Gabriel was well aware of the situatedness of his perspective: 'it's a white, middle class, ex-public schoolboy, domesticated, English person observing his own reactions from afar. It seemed impossible to me that the South Africans had let him be killed when there had been so much international publicity about his imprisonment.'[21]

Stephen Biko died in 1977, as a result of being tortured in the apartheid prison system. Even more explicitly than Nazism, South African apartheid legislated for turning racial hatred into oppression and murder. So it was hardly a difficult target for artists. But in 1980, the extent to which the South African state was crushing opposition, as well as decreeing the majority of its people to be of a lower level of humanity, was not as widely known as might be expected. Further, a significant number of politicians in many countries around the world (and not just the then UK-ruling Conservative Party) were not inclined to disrupt very 'healthy' economic ties. Gabriel's song, seven minutes on the album, nearly nine on the German version and single, became an epic symbol of Western liberal anger at the persistent survival of external support for the apartheid state. It was a simple track lyrically, recounting Biko's fate in prison but also evoking the culpability and responsibility of people outside South Africa for events within. For example, musicians and sportspeople would insist that their continuing to play in the country was not a form of tacit support. The 1980s saw a range of grudgingly offered international sanctions on that country and a belated disengagement by the cricketers and rock musicians who had continued to perform in South Africa. This helped the drive to overturn the regime from within. Musically, the song vaguely suggests African circular rythms over the beat and bar structure of rock, ironically continuing progressive rock's turn from the blues roots of rock in so doing. It does this through Gabriel's unchanging drum program track and interspersed, fragmentary drum kit runs. The track is framed with uncredited vocal music we are led to hear as African, the real Africa in some way, but then ends with the didactic finality of a last 'gated' salvo of drum kit hits.[22]

Stephen Biko stood out in the bloody history of racist oppression in South Africa because his activism offered a vision of a peaceful future, one that would begin by making everyone inside the country, and beyond, aware of what was going on under the apartheid system. For Gabriel, Biko himself had managed to convey this 'in a way that polarised politics often doesn't'.[23] The sense of knowledge as utopian possibility is what would drive Gabriel's involvement not just in Amnesty International but also in the Witness campaign, which promotes and publicizes the photographing and filming of violent attacks around the world in order to expose the true face of power that underpins overt political discourse – hence the importance for Gabriel's career and work of the line 'And the eyes of the world are watching now', which closes the song part of the track. From this point on, Gabriel was politically engaged, part of a global political community, as heard through the dual grounding of 'Biko' in folk song and electronics (the latter destined to be a much more authentic shared global culture, albeit not yet in 1980).

The two parts of this album connect the individual in urban society not to his fellow citizen, who is often entangled in normativity, but to the oppressed everywhere. Gabriel was not suggesting an equivalence between obsessed loners and the lethally oppressed, but he was making links between what gets left outside, as a way of addressing how people in the West perceive what is around them. In short, most people tend to ignore the world beyond the remit of law, where there are practices that are not subject to any control, or where people are not in a position to benefit from expectations within capitalist production and reproduction. In the third *Peter Gabriel*, real borders are there to be undermined, and so should any moves towards internal policing.

Local social control, even under the would-be benevolence of consumerist capitalism, is the danger, more than any apparent or publicized dangers.[24]

The connection between sounds from 'outside' and social marginalization, exclusion and oppression that Gabriel developed in 'Biko' expanded on 1982's *Peter Gabriel*, his fourth album (subtitled 'Security' in the U.S.). But Gabriel's use of outsiderness or 'otherness' altered dramatically as he moved from a conception of the radicality of exclusion to a view and aural expression of shared community through the embrace of sound and ideas from cultures other than the one from which he sprang. The album begins with a dual salvo of percussion-dominated tracks, which serve to open up a prospect of a world community through rhythm. 'The Rhythm of the Heat', inspired by psychologist Carl Jung's visit to Sudan, is a minimalist track, driven by electronics and the Ekome Dance Company's drums, amid other percussion and non-rock instrumentation – a sound that dominates this album and the succeeding soundtracks that Gabriel worked on through the decade. The narrator looks out on a dusty desert landscape as the pulsing mounts in volume and presence. For all that the liner notes specify a location, the place of this track is amorphous: it is the desert, it is the land as geology, and ultimately the site of geology intruding into self. As the narrator notes his surroundings, the rhythm gradually takes over, a mineral pulsing in tune with the being of Gabriel's stand-in: 'The Rhythm is around me / The Rhythm has control / The Rhythm is inside me / The Rhythm has my soul', with the end of the verse almost shouted. Chants pepper the track, suggesting a voice, or voices, emerging from nature – an environmental voice.

The whole moves towards the union between spirit and land, a Romantic, exotic vision in sound and image. 'The Rhythm of the Heat' indicates an outsider moving towards the inside, the inner being of a foreign land now become if not familiar, then at least capable of acknowledgement and acceptance. Potential danger turns into harmonious living. While the track has an autonomous existence, it is hard not to read it as a reflection on Gabriel's own immersion into musics and rhythms from far beyond Anglo-centred rock. As well as stating it was a 'Ghanaian war dance' that had inspired the crescendo of the track, Gabriel has praised the idea of borrowing itself, in an interview with Richard Cook, saying,

> I think theft of all types is very important to any music that is alive . . . If I hear original rhythm patterns from elsewhere that motivate me, that I wouldn't have come across in rock music, then I'll make use of them.[25]

More than a biographical account, the use of a narrator in the song transformed the track into a self-reflective, formalist state-ment of what it means to take on 'otherness' and bring it close.

The exoticist is always on a quest to find the other and learn its ways, sometimes for nefarious purposes, at others as a form of benevolent yet still condescending usage. What Gabriel was hearing at this point was the prospect of something like world music, a unifying but not closed system of musical transfer and inspiration, and as far as he was concerned, the exchange of musical ideas is everywhere, a global process in its own right, observing that 'in Bali, if they hear disco music from pirated cassettes it can be incorporated into the gamelan music. It's not just one way.'[26] The issues around the use of non-Western musics will be discussed more fully in the next chapter and beyond, but Gabriel's outlook requires a reflection on the idea of exoticism and on Edward Said's idea of 'Orientalism', elaborated in the book of that name published in 1978, more or less contemporane-ously with the arrival of *Peter Gabriels*.[27] For many centuries, Said argued, Western thinkers have sought to understand 'the Orient', some with genuine fascination and immersion, others with more cynical motives. Almost all had characterized an array of different places and historical societies as 'the Orient', as an other to be understood. Behind this characterization lay a set of shared presumptions held by 'good' exoticists and colonial adminstrators alike.

Over time, writers have tried making a more subtle distinction than that made by Said, and others have overstated it, almost imagining that Westerners were inevitably doomed to such politically semi-racist stereotyping. Said himself was clear that this was not his intent and that we should not all turn in on our own societies.[28] Instead it should be the duty of anyone interested in what they thought of as a 'different' society to make sure that they do engage with it, and try to overcome the biases that come from their own socialization. This, I would argue, is what we can clearly hear in Peter Gabriel's work, and in fact we can read his work from the early 1980s onward as a parallel theorization of how place, music and identity combine or brush up against one another.

In order to conceive of Gabriel's explorations in music from Africa, in particular, we need to reconsider the term 'exoticist'. The exoticist loves cultures for being different, and in so doing characterizes them into a position of otherness where only he has the power to understand them. Over the years, many journalists have wondered in this vein about Gabriel, or anyone interested in music from outside their own localized genres. But the exoticist can be someone much more interesting, and can get past many of the potential problems of condescension or expropriation. Charles Forsdick argues that the prominent pro-exoticist writer and traveller Victor Segalen (1878–1919) shows us a more complex way of thinking of the practice and the term itself – one that I think fits Gabriel perfectly. Forsdick writes,

Segalen's exoticism [is] not Eurocentric but Eurocentrifugal
– [it] is an individual, early twentieth-century reaction to an
experience of the world now increasingly termed 'postcolonial': an experience of declining cultural difference, of the
articulate other, and of the subsequently fragmented, unstable
self.[29]

We have already seen that Gabriel was embracing fragmentation
as part of the contemporary social and individual condition,
and we need to bear in mind that this is how he has continued
to approach all locations and relations, wherever they are in the
world, and that the most 'exotic' thing is the self. Through the
prism of the hybrid, othered self, the music and musicians of
places other than British rock were and are only ever as exotic and
other as Gabriel himself, or his evolving idea of England. Tracking
this political/psychological/philosophical journey through the
rest of his work is how I will show this creative 'exotic' view to be
present in it.

For now, with this characterization in mind, I intend to return
to what we actually have 'in front of us' aurally, and what it tries
to communicate, in a self-conscious and aware fashion, about
locatedness outside of rock norms, including when a full encounter with the 'other' culture is staged. This was only beginning on
this *Peter Gabriel* (1982), an album that was still vigorously trying to
reposition and manoeuvre a Peter Gabriel into open ground. 'San
Jacinto' sees Gabriel sing-talking again, over a minimalist loop,
percussion gradually mounting, building to the first chorus part
at 3 minutes, 30 seconds. The song is about a contrast between
traditional Native American ways and consumer culture, which
awaits at the completion of the destruction of other cultures in
the building of the u.s. The central character of the song, whom
I take also to be an outsider being initiated, talks of how the
'medicine man lead me up through town', and is brought to a

place beyond the solid yet artificial life of now, and for the second time on the opening two tracks, the narrator leaves his body behind to merge with something bigger. The initial temptation is to hear the insidious voice of hippy icon Carlos Castaneda, with his cod-mystic journeys of discovery, but something more critical and speculative stands in the way, in the form the lyrics take. It may just be a lucky accident, but the lyrics are disjointed phrases connected by dashes, strongly suggesting the writing of William Burroughs, inventor (with Brion Gysin) of the cut-up method of collaged writing and a noted exoticist and experimenter in his day. Most specifically it is the book *The Yage Letters* (1963) that is recalled, the epistolary account of Burroughs traipsing around South America for a mystical experience to be released through shamanic plant consumption (in the song this is where 'the poison bite and darkness take my sight').[30]

Both Gabriel and Burroughs were strongly exoticist, fascinated by potential discovery outside their familiar territories, internal or geographic, trying to jolt themselves and their listeners/readers into a place different from their starting point. Both have also romanticized the nobility of 'other' cultures, but did so in ways that maintained a sense of external perspective that was not about full appropriation or even incorporation (other than in the sense of creative borrowing). The rhythmical, global side of the album returns in its closing track, 'The Kiss of Life', a less successful imagining, with multiple percussions, chanting, arousing finale and a joyous dance feel. The lyrical focus on some sort of goddess or witch figure identified as a 'big woman', dancing, vivacious and full of spirit, makes this an awkward moment, as Gabriel indulges in a very rare moment of cultural, casually sexist misappropriation in some imaginary ritual. What begins as an attempt at a liberatory dance moment, as something more open, more celebratory, away from the more wary themes and tones of this fourth *Peter Gabriel*, falls flat.

In between the opening statements of the album and the jollity of the end lay another burgeoning obsession of Gabriel: the highly mediatized nature of commodity/consumer culture. As media began targeting the people as masses, and simplifying accordingly, Britain and the u.s. (under Margaret Thatcher and Ronald Reagan respectively) were attempting to lead the world into the dominion of private wealth accumulation as public good. The wealth of a few would create aspiration; this would be backed up fiscally in terms of lowering taxation, which benefited high earners more, supposedly stimulating individuals and the economy to ever higher achievement. Into this world came not only the desktop computer, the yuppie and mtv but also public relations, image development and the use of the media to earn money directly. 'I Have the Touch' turns Gabriel's suspicion of bourgeois conformity into an attack on those who create and benefit from capitalist and media exploitation. The businessman narrator is on the move, loving the buzz of capital. The 'contact' that is all he craves is the making of business contacts, the building of networks, the frottage of a mass of humanity ready to supply him with profit. Ultimately, the psychopath has found his place, and it is not at the edge of town, but in charge of the economy, in charge of fashioning new urban and commercial behaviours. 'Lay Your Hands on Me' addresses what would come to be a common topic of critique in music of the 1980s: the mediatized, stadium preacher. As well as this direct target, Gabriel was again reflecting on his own practice as a rock performer and the megalomania that comes from self-belief generated through the fandom of others. In performance, on the 'Security' tour, Gabriel used this song as the basis for his crowdsurfing, as he would drop into the audience (as he had done in different ways since the early days of Genesis) and be held aloft as he continued to sing, making himself vulnerable at exactly the time he sought the touch of the converts. The two remaining tracks work on the process of psychological learning, the self-awareness of limits, and so extend the musing on the external subjectivities of the previous, third, *Peter Gabriel*.

The attempt at locatedness was stronger than ever on 1982's *Peter Gabriel*, but also more diffuse – a sense of inner and outer space combining, if not exactly merging. The inner became more open, the outer then presented itself as open, and Gabriel went rushing in to these openings. From being on the outside, his music and narrators addressed, used, met and reflected on the outside. More than this, the music moved ever further not just from the glades of Albion or the subways of New York, but also from the globalizing of Western rock that MTV, digital recording and faster communications were about to spread ever more rapidly around the world (those very changes would draw Gabriel's music back into their realm). Gabriel's interest in cultural authenticity was a resistance to that globalizing pressure, however easy it might be to dismiss as romanticized, even condescending. His use of technology, mass media, and awareness of the power of what is most new, most appropriate to the globalized future, made his turn to the complete world of music much more interesting, and authentic in some sort of postmodern, post-identity world, as did his practical involvement in promoting music from around the world on a global scale through WOMAD, Real World and collaborations with many musicians.

4 REAL WORLD

In the course of the 1980s, Peter Gabriel extended his forays in non-Western music into several domains, continuing to expand his interest in politics, jointly setting up the World of Music, Arts and Dance organization (WOMAD), and establishing his studio at Box Mill (12 km from Bath in southwest England), which would become Real World Studios, home of Real World Records, a major force in the promotion of world music. While I continue to track Gabriel chronologically, I am interested here in the musical definition, mobilization and promotion of world music, and in terms of Gabriel's own work, I will look at his engagement with music from around the world from the early 1980s up to 1989. This culminated, in output terms, in his soundtrack for Martin Scorsese's film *The Last Temptation of Christ* (1988), entitled *Passion* and released in 1989, which was accompanied by the compilation *Passion: Sources*.

In 1980, Peter Gabriel's 'Biko' began its career as an international protest song, though banned in Biko's native South Africa – the apartheid-based state was particularly unnerved by the sleeve of the single, which showed numerous wounds to Biko's body as well as displaying the lyrics, with Gabriel later describing it as 'a calling card announcing I was interested and prepared to get involved'.[1] At the same time, Gabriel began his parallel career as a curator and promoter of music from outside Europe, forming WOMAD with Bob Hooton, Mark Kidel, Stephen Pritchard, Martin

Elbourne, Jonathan Arthur and Thomas Brooman, the last of whom would act as artistic director of the festival until 2008. Gabriel's cultural politicization took place against a backdrop of the right-wing Conservative government of Margaret Thatcher – no supporter of anti-apartheid ideas – and racial tensions that had simmered and fizzled in the late 1970s, manifested in black protest riots such as those in Brixton in 1981. This tension was fed by the growth of a seething racist skinhead subculture, lured away from their origins in being fans of ska in the 1960s by the extreme right-wing National Front party, avant-garde of a new generation of violence-oriented skinheads, which represented a real day-to-day threat, while the police helped fan flames of tension in black areas of English cities by persistently stopping and searching young black men. In terms of popular music, the Britain Gabriel lived in was starting to become conscious of black musics, particularly reggae, and this helped the country notice it was already not a homogeneous mass and laid the foundations for non-Western music to get noticed.

The very first WOMAD was held from 16 to 18 July 1982, in Shepton Mallet, Somerset, not far from either the recently acquired Box studio, or indeed from Solsbury Hill, and featured 'over 60 artists from over 20 countries', according to publicity for the event. The line-up included rock bands who were then popular in Britain (such as Simple Minds and Echo & the Bunnymen) as well as many musicians from outside Europe, including The Drummers of Burundi, Shankar and the Ekome Dance Company. This concession to commercial wisdom did not pay off, even with a decent attendance of 15,000 people, as the first festival was inexpertly run and a financial disaster – costs soared and the publicity was poorly done. Genesis came to the rescue and played a one-off concert – with Gabriel singing – to alleviate the debts Gabriel had accrued. This event, 'Six of the Best', took place at Milton Keynes Bowl on 2 October 1982. Although the set was predominantly made up of songs from Gabriel's time in the band, it also included his song that is most likely about leaving it ('Solsbury Hill'), and, more strangely, Gabriel played drums while Phil Collins sang on the post-Gabriel Genesis hit 'Turn It On Again'. Not so much a return as a send-off, the help provided by Genesis would see WOMAD able to restart, and over the years it not only became viable but spread globally, being staged in many countries outside Britain, including Abu Dhabi, Australia, Spain, Chile, the USA, Singapore and South Africa, with several events happening every year.[2]

At the time, this was an unusual festival. In the early 1980s, in Britain at least, there was nothing like the festival culture of the early twenty-first century. There was Glastonbury, with 25,000 people in attendance (as opposed to 135,000 today), there was the Notting Hill carnival, and there were free festivals. The politicized, 'conscious' festival began to spread as a tool for raising awareness of social issues. The 1980s saw left-wing groups organize internationally themed events, as had been common for some time in communist-run cities in Western Europe, and indeed in the Soviet bloc. As a large version of what is now common as a boutique festival, WOMAD pioneered not only in content but also in form, in offering

> Continuous performances by artists from four continents. Two outdoor stages. Two stages in circus big-tops. Large selection of non-western foods available. Market fair. Continuous programme of films. Covered exhibitions of world arts and crafts. Music workshops. Inflatables. Surprises![3]

It further promised both 'new and traditional' arts, clearly indicating its mission of cultural and aesthetic mixing. The music festivals of the late 1960s and early '70s had of course attempted to be self-contained, fugitive spaces for their duration, but WOMAD sought to be more than music plus backdrop. Instead, its multiple nature in mounting arts 'from around the world' was intended to be explicitly holistic. This festival would be self-contained, a miniature society, open to existing and future communities to form and cement exchanges. It is important to note that the festival, with artistic director Brooman at its helm and with Gabriel heavily involved, represented a multimedia event in material form, anticipating Gabriel's later media-crossing artworks. The reference to 'new and traditional' was also carefully proposed, in not wishing to render 'other' music or arts archaic. Five years before the term 'world music' was spawned as a commercial branding, 'world arts and crafts' quietly became part of a more traditional, rock-style event.

World music is a highly contentious term, with scholars and critics connecting the idea to debates about colonialism, imperialism, condescension, cultural openness and interaction, authenticity, exploitation and promotion. Many 'world' musicians are conscious of the contentious nature of where their albums are likely to be filed. Most music identified as being part of the 'genre' existed before its coining, but also, beyond and before it were Peter Gabriel's multiple encounters with 'the world of music', whether in WOMAD, his use of African music, or his collaborations with musicians such as Youssou N'Dour or Nusrat Fateh Ali Khan, underway since the 1980s (Gabriel first heard N'Dour in concert in 1983 and was set on working with him from that point). In other words, Gabriel's primary position with regard to world music is that of practitioner, of being involved in the practice of music from beyond his genre or locality. The *Passion* album is, from start to finish, an exercise in making a hybrid global music, devised to bring musics from different places into a new hybrid form. This is perhaps why Gabriel's idealism has been open to criticism – as it has not been couched in anxiety, at least not at first, although by the end of the decade he was more self-conscious of his position

Poster for the first World of Music and Dance (WOMAD) festival, co-organized by Peter Gabriel with Thomas Brooman, Bob Hooton, Mark Kidel, Stephen Pritchard, Martin Elbourne and Jonathan Arthur.

as Western, global star, with his role including the financing of many strands of music from Africa and Asia in particular.

Before getting to the vexed question of what to do about or with 'world music', let us review some of the 'problems' of Western, mostly anglophone rock stars, as they discovered through a teary eye the plight and bravery of Africa, the terrible human rights abuses around the world, and staged an endless stadium charity trudge through the second part of the decade. It all began in earnest with Band Aid's 'Do They Know It's Christmas?', released in late 1984 in order to raise awareness of and money for Ethiopia, which was in the midst of a two-year-long famine that would kill hundreds of thousands of people.[4] This was followed by Live Aid, staged in London and New York on 13 July 1985. Although later years have exposed problems regarding what actually happened to the money raised as a result of these initiatives, it is mostly on the motives of those involved that criticism centred at the time, and since. After Live Aid, a familiar cast of multimillionaire, mostly white, rock stars would play some hits to a massive TV audience as well as to the crowd gathered in the stadium, while maybe offering a couple of platitudes about how terrible things are in 'the place this event is about'. Curiously, as one of very few Western musicians explicitly interested in Africa, with connections to African bands and solo artists, no one thought to ask Peter Gabriel to be involved in helping to organize Live Aid, or even to play. For all the criticizable limits of WOMAD's push on 'world music', at least a good few non-Europeans were there, as opposed to none at Live Aid (while admitting that Freddie Mercury, born in Zanzibar, offered one notable exception, his music never ranged outside Western forms).

Further examples in Britain were to be found in the politicization of rock that had happened alongside punk and reggae, adding to a feeling of momentum towards political engagement as part of what a pop musician did. While some punk bands veered to the extreme Right, many of those inspired by punk and reggae, its accomplice in anti-conformism, made their left-wing politics known. The decade also saw Rock Against Racism (from 1976 on), strong support for the striking mineworkers, and the Red Wedge movement (which started in 1985 and looked to harness social unrest and transform it into social change, including through support for the centre-left Labour Party). These groupings, as well as events organized by 'revolutionary' socialist movements, were spreading the idea of art and music as authentically international, genuinely communal. Peter Gabriel was somewhere in the middle of this, more of a radical liberal than a full-blown leftist. This would manifest in his active, high-profile membership and advocacy of Amnesty International and Witness.

The term 'world music' is so heavily freighted, it might seem desirable to leave it out entirely, but clearly this is not possible in the case of a Western rock artist with so many extensions into other musics. In any case, Gabriel has received criticism that closely parallels that of the whole idea of world music. For Gabriel, the term 'world music' was and is full of meaning, an expression of a truly global reality about the potential of all music to be heard by all: 'music is a universal language,' he said, writing in 2008 of WOMAD and Thomas Brooman's contribution to its growth.[5] If the choice to listen to non-rock, non-Western music is an aesthetic one, it is a philosophically aesthetic one for Gabriel, as it contains a political belief in the harmony of humanity, at least in potential. It contains a belief that a particular set of creative activities, differing in their social role across a range of societies, can be communicated across borders, differences, practical limitations or oppression. This is the utopian side of a belief in the value of 'other' musics, whose 'passionate spirit', said Gabriel in 1989, crosses cultural boundaries.[6] It is also a statement that the 'otherness' of actual others is not definitive or determining, nor is it an anatagonistic choice or a potential danger. So, we could say that Gabriel's overall belief in the universality of music, or musical practice and activity, has manifested mostly through direct musical production, and this has led to the simple actions of playing, listening, releasing, producing, collaborating with musicians from cultures outside Europe.

For Philip V. Bohlman, world music is very broad, covering many types of music, produced in different ways for an array of purposes and situations, plenty of which mirror the production of pop, rock, classical and even experimental musics that are globally familiar. In fact, 'the world of world music has no boundaries, therefore access to world music is open to all.'[7] This sounds very positive – it is a category that is wide open, inviting, open to listeners in unpredictable contexts, and seems to be highly democratic. This openness, however, risks leading to homogenization, under the aegis of an almost totally vacuous idea. It would then lead to exactly the opposite effect of that intended. In removing the specificity of particular musicians or styles and in lumping everyone outside mainstream Western-originated genres into one mass, it could even reduce their commercial reach. It could also affect much-desired authenticity, as this new generic category could actually encourage musicians to homogenize styles, aiming to match a kind of hyper-generic expectation on the part of labels and 'other' listeners (Western listeners can be 'other' too in the context of listening to world music).

It is no accident that world music arrived when it did, in the late 1980s. The latest wave of globalization was well under way, even with the Internet merely nascent at the time. Capitalist neoliberalism was spreading as a political model, accompanied by the growth of world-covering corporations. Not least among these latter were the manufacturers of music products, both recordings and hardware. Rock and pop music had become a *technology* of globalization; not just a beneficiary or possible victim, but a driver of it. Bohlman specifically says that 'world music is inseparable from another equally difficult to define phenomenon of our age, globalization.'[8] Whereas rock and pop, sung primarily in English and from a very limited number of countries, had helped create a mediatized and ideologically insidious globalization, world music appeared as a category at a time when global distribution was already possible, when the tendrils of the 'music business' were capable of reaching deeply into the loam of all societies. World music would be able to benefit from this (which is exactly the mission of WOMAD and Real World), but prior to that, it offered itself as an alternative to the prevailing top-down homogenizing of Anglo pop and rock. In so doing, it risked becoming hostage to the reductive drive of a business based on genre, so that we could end up perceiving a range of diverse musics as being part of a single phenomenon.

There is a significant point tucked away behind the simple one of creating sameness where there was difference, and that is the opposition between universalism and relativism, an issue that haunts world music and ethnomusicology. Universalism supposes that everyone has a shared humanity that is, at its core, the same everywhere. In musical terms, this idea can be used for systems of tonality, the inevitability of human musicality, the omnipresence of rhythm, or beliefs that music has a role to play for everyone, if we could just hear it properly. Relativism posits the opposite: everything you see is a product of a particular time and place – so there is no such thing as definitive tonality, we cannot attribute a single musicality or rhythmic feeling to humans. In fact, we cannot speak necessarily meaningfully of 'humans', but need to identify the ways in which a group has been constructed by their context, history and pre-existing institutions and ideas. World music has to negotiate between these ways of seeing the world, and it must maintain this sense of navigating the hazards of reducing a particular music to just being part of a single 'patchwork' or

of imagining local musics to be so individual that they could not
logically be 'heard' by other cultural groups.

This is why I think that the idea of global citizenship can
be very productive, with its sense of responsibility to the world
as a whole, a single world, but one made of diverse elements
that cannot be reduced. This sense of being a citizen who must
participate, as opposed to sit back and only criticize, has Peter
Gabriel as an exemplary model. The citizen both benefits from
and is responsible for how (in this case) music is received. In other
words, the more actively either musicians or listeners engage
with something like world music, the less chance there is that the
problems that can arise (of homogenization, condescension, loss
of specificity, exploitation) can be used in the service of a blanket
critique of any and all engagement. Gabriel's liberalism leans
heavily on his idea that 'music is the first universal language', as he
told Terry Wogan in 1987, hence it has a capacity to communicate
ideas and at least contribute to the prospect of change.[9] This
engagement would be quite different to that of the inventors of
the term 'world music', and neither would it fall into the facile
belief that 'it's all just music' and therefore we should forget about
genres altogether. This sort of wishing away has its political corol-
lary in liberal quietism (where you would accept all that happens,
in the belief that fundamentally the system is fine), or a kind of
alienated subjectivity with the core belief that decisions are all
based on personal taste or, worse, expert listening capacity. In any
case, political or philosophical niceties were far from the termino-
logical assembly that first devised the idea of world music:

> The expression 'World Music' acquired currency in Europe
> and North America after a meeting in 1987 of concert promot-
> ers, journalists, musicians, and independent record company
> owners in The Empress of Russia, a pub in Islington,
> London.[10]

This seems to have been a cynical land grab, while claiming to have been a way to help musicians have a higher profile. Either way, it was undeniably a capitalization of music from non-Western and / or non-pop / rock settings. From the perspective of thirty years later, it is no more or less an invention than any other genre to be found in a record shop or that exists as guiding pretext for an online forum. But 'world music' makes claims and reductions that, say, the terms 'metal' or 'rap' do not. There is a claim in world music, made by its producers, audiences and record labels, of access to something authentic, something outside the market system, pure, closer to the source of music. At the same time, this properness can all be swirled and stirred together, a thousand styles in one genre. For the ethnomusicologist Steven Feld, 'it is as a commercial marketing label that "world music" is now most commonly placed.'[11] Beneath the label lies 'the idea that musics originate from all world regions, cultures, and historical formations. "World music" thus circulates broadly in a liberal, relativist field of discourse.'[12] Leaving aside the relativist question, which is only one half of the 'liberal' presumption in 'world music' (liberalism is complex, too), it is clear that world music ends up carrying a lot of responsibility for the prospects or difficulties in achieving universal, harmonious living, either through sameness or difference. World music becomes the real to the fake of Western rock stars, and the record companies profit by playing the two against each other, within a globalized economy they helped create and continue to maintain, even as newer corporations reap the benefits today. This desired realness is one message clearly sent out by the name Real World – as the rock critic Franck Buioni writes, it is a name developed as a contrast to Disney World, the paradigm of capitalist, Western ideologizing.[13] Just as clearly, we could see world music as exactly the opposite of realness, a simulation modelled as real.

This 'realness', or its opposite – the refusal to accept the claims of authenticity put forward on behalf of selected

musicians as part of world music – often leads to debates about
purity, where authenticity is presumed to be about unchanging
tradition. World music itself has a very strong component of
mixing, of fusion, for better or worse, and instead of remind-
ing us that some musics are more real than others, it can just
as easily work as a mode of understanding all music as being
compromised by historical, contextual factors, and aesthetic
mixing. The Congolese performer Papa Wemba was one artist
picked up by Real World, and he played with Peter Gabriel on
record and in concert, with his own band. A mainstay of music
in the Democratic Republic of the Congo since the late 1960s, he
brought into his music a Cuban influence (not unusual in north-
western or central Africa), but also rock 'n' roll, Jimi Hendrix and
Bob Dylan. Far from diverting Papa Wemba from the path of
static localism, the extended encounter with Peter Gabriel only
added a turn to the spiral of cross-cultural influence.[14] This example also highlights a certain limit in English-language discourse
about world music, because in French culture and criticism,
musical hybridity has gone hand in hand with postcolonial, dias-
poric populations, long before being categorized by country in
record shops or the virtual racks of online stores.

There had been occasional Western forays into non-Western
music before the 1980s, though on a much smaller scale than
the colossal influence and appropriation of Western rock by
musicians outside that zone. In the 1950s, a few composers hit
commercial gold with their 'exotica', most notably Martin Denny,
who released an album of that name, and the more experimental Les Baxter. Both made albums which were a pot-pourri of
different musics, with particular instruments such as moderately
unfamiliar 'other' percussion or wind instruments featuring
strongly. The musics from elsewhere were reconfigured into
easy listening, with just a tinge of foreign spice. Les Baxter went
further, inventing notional pan-tribal musics, on albums such as

Ritual of the Savage (1951), making literal Igor Stravinsky's similar
attempt in 1913 at tapping into the Dionysian tribal beat of the
world, in *The Rite of Spring*. Through the 1960s, what was not yet
called 'lounge' music would summon flavours from around the
world, even if more at home in conjuring pastiches of European
culture; or you could always go further, with albums such as Bert
Kaempfert's *A Swingin' Safari* (1962), home to 'Wimoweh', among
other borderline-racist musical moves. For its critics, world music
was not much better than this swathe of bourgeois toe-tapping
into distant waters, as it was equally processed and stereotyped by
encounters with the West – through its naming, categorizing, and
commercial interaction with Western musicians.

Glimpses of Gabriel's mode of encounter with the expanded
world of music appear in occasional moments of earlier rock
exoticism, notably on the part of Brian Jones and George
Harrison, or, better, on the part of the Master Musicians of
Joujouka and Ravi Shankar, respectively, with the latter a major
influence on George Harrison from 1965 on. The two cases
above are far from the same, but represent in different ways the
problems that may arise when wealthy, already global musicians
encounter, translate or promote artists far from those influential
heights. As well as the potential for diminishing the originality
that was the first point of interest, there is also the issue of
'positional' dominance, as Timothy D. Taylor has it.[15] The 'world'
musicians, such as the Master Musicians, would benefit, if at all,
in a kind of vassal role, from the patronage of Brian Jones, thanks
to his membership of The Rolling Stones. Shankar, on the other
hand, was very well known and his music well travelled by the
time he inspired a range of mid-1960s British rock groups, as he
had been playing his classical sitar music around the world since
the mid-1950s. For all the difficulty in defining or accepting world
music, it has to be said that Shankar really did the work that world
music as a label was designed for – spreading the word through

direct performance – so certainly, of the two most high-profile cases in the late 1960s, the connection between Shankar and Harrison began from a much more equitable starting point. It also tied in to the broader phenomenon of the 1960s counterculture questing after 'spirituality' as part of its rejection of capitalism and imperialist wars such as the one being staged in Vietnam, and rock stars and hippies all sought 'wisdom' that tied into a pan-cosmic and blurry view of the world's cultures.

A few fusion groups took a route that went further out than merging rock and jazz, with Santana and Osibisa exemplars of this 1970s 'genre'.[16] The practices of these two groups, with their multiple cultural reference points, took away the question of hier-archy, as the groups did not 'find an other' and then use them as backing music, ornamentation, or have them as a secondary part-ner. In this, they more closely resembled many of the groups that ended up on Real World's label – combining ranges of traditional sounds with references to contemporary music, regional and international, into a type of music the people in the West could hear either as pop or as traditional. For Real World, and perhaps the idea of world music in general, either would work. It seems clear that on many occasions what was being dealt with were musics that came from hybridity (just like rock, or pop, or jazz) and did not grow as indigeneous or endogenous objects, fixed and awaiting discovery and transplantation to a Western hothouse.

The leading ethnomusicologist Laurent Aubert has argued that world music is 'essentially intercultural experience in the form of popular and contemporary music'.[17] This type of expe-rience, if not common in late 1960s or 1970s Europe and North America, was certainly known, as evidenced through the commer-cial success of the examples cited above (with the exception of the delayed release of the Master Musicians LP). Europeans were also familiar with the music of other European nations, genres, traditions, and were gradually becoming aware of Jamaican styles ınitially through calypso's commercialization).[18] Such intercultural exchange mirrored social changes, thanks to what Aubert calls 'migratory flows'.[19] In France in particular, the audience for what would come to be known as 'world music' was often a relocated 'native' one, and the spread of 'musiques du monde' (note the plural) about as far from a neo-imperialist impulse as could be imagined. France has been home to many African artists, and also to bands that were formed in order to combine music from different cultural traditions. Like Britain, this multicultural, home-grown culture owes a debt to where empire went, where slaves were transported to and from, but there is only so far such history delimits the possibility of cross-cultural hybrid musics, without removing creative agency from artists.

Artistic control and freedom is, of course, one of the major practical, as well as theoretical, issues when non-Western musicians work with established Western stars. In 1986, Paul Simon brought out his highly successful album *Graceland*, controversially going against the widespread boycott of South Africa in order to work with many musicians from that country, bringing in traditional and more contemporary pop elements. Gabriel was not in favour of the refusal to work with South African musicians while the apartheid regime was in place, but, unlike Simon, Gabriel adhered to it in order to follow the lead of those in the country:

> the cultural boycott is something I have a lot of problems with . . . Art has always been connected with cultural change so that if you cut off artistic communication you slow the process down. However, I do support the boycott, although I think it's wrong, because we are asked to by the people involved, the black people of South Africa. I took the decision out of respect for their struggle.[20]

Steven Feld sees *Graceland* as posing the paradigmatic set of problems for Western rock stars in using African music and musicians – in short, it is a *use*, and the star retains ownership, no matter how far individuals, organizations and groups are credited and paid properly.[21] Is there a way around this problem? Is the Westerner always going to arrive in a dominant position, the 'subaltern' kept from recognition in their own right? Correctly, we should be suspicious of the increased likelihood of such under-attentiveness in the context of a world music that flattens out differences. Timothy D. Taylor asserts that whatever Gabriel does, 'his positionality as a westerner and as a male star in the music industry means that his musics are always appropriative in some ways.'[22] In short, Gabriel was born into an exploitative, only recently post-colonizing country, so is caught within that structure, from which he benefits in terms of cultural and financial capital. That is feasible, if determinist, but, as Gabriel can do nothing about it, hardly a worthwhile or meaningful challenge for him.

Feld's doubt about 'world music' is that world music misrepresents cultures, sometimes exploits them culturally, more occasionally financially, and flattens the difference it was supposedly brought into existence to maintain. He uses 'schizophonia', the word coined by R. Murray Schafer, to identify 'sounds [that] have increasingly been mediated, split from their sources'.[23] In Gabriel's borrowings, he has been able to perform a type of 'schizophonia' that is not abusive or exploitative, but the source of creative hybridity, as we will see with the *Passion* album. Gabriel's involvement with 'world music' is highly proactive and shows a way of using dis-location as a creative multiplier of possibilities.

The only safe way to avoid all criticism in a politically charged area of cross-cultural, international collaboration, particularly if one partner is personally wealthy, is to not bother. But the global citizen starts from a position of responsibility, not isolationism, and so Gabriel works with non-Western musicians because the musical citizenship extends beyond the world of Western rock musicians.

As WOMAD's fortunes improved, Gabriel honed some of the sounds of the fourth *Peter Gabriel* album and added some new tracks in the same atmospheric vein for Alan Parker's film *Birdy* (film 1984, album 1985). While the main character's position is close to those featured in Gabriel's earlier albums, in being on the edge, and looking to get further out, the album is very much a collection of parts that work better while accompanying the film. Aware of that possibility recurring, Gabriel worked the soundtrack of *The Last Temptation of Christ* into the double album *Passion* over a period of several months, eventually releasing it in 1989. Nonetheless, the rhythmic focus of *Passion* was already developing in the collaborations and freshly recast tracks of *Birdy*, with the latter a kind of electronic template for further expanding the range of musical styles. The reimaginings of *Deutsches Album* had begun the process of stripping back and altering the sounds of the fourth *Peter Gabriel*, and on *Birdy* these float free as pulsing, droning, beating ambiences.

The idea of Gabriel making the soundtrack for *The Last Temptation of Christ* had been in gestation since before *Birdy*, with Scorsese first approaching Gabriel about the project in 1983. In the interim period leading up to the film's release, Gabriel had substantially expanded his list of contacts of musicians in Africa and Asia, many of whom would go on to feature on the soundtrack to *The Last Temptation*. Scorsese had been listening to Moroccan music and looked to Gabriel to expand on that interest, having been inspired by the sounds of the fourth *Peter Gabriel*, particularly 'The Rhythm of the Heat'. Scorsese saw this combination of sounds extending across many countries to be capable of producing a deep and therefore more affecting sound, saying (in 1987, before the film was out) that 'Peter took many of the rhythms from Turkey, Greece, Armenia, North Africa and Senegal, mixing them together to make the music as primal as possible.'[24] Ultimately, the director was interested in how 'the rhythms [Gabriel] uses reflect the primitive, and his vocals reflect the sublime'.[25] I have tried to show that Gabriel had a subtler sense of what he was doing and how he related to the world of music he was accessing for the soundtrack and much of his work in the 1980s. This is not to say that a critical reading cannot be done, not least when *Passion* is considered alongside the compilation *Passion: Sources*, released the same day as *Passion*, as one of the five inaugural releases on Real World, on 5 June 1989.

Passion begins with a drone, which is soon joined by the keening of the Armenian duduk. As we approach one minute into the piece, the percussion begins, heavy with portent, to be joined by more of a constellation of rhythm devices. 'The Feeling Begins' layers traditional instruments, sampler (mirroring traditional sounds, and also making sounds that had never been part of any existing culture), keyboards, non-Western percussion, and guitar (sparsely used on the album, and even when present is treated and not clearly audible as electric guitar), so there is almost nothing by way of tuned Western instrumentation on the album. When the piano makes its rare appearance, it has a dramatic and unexpectedly disorienting feel. *Passion* is replete with many percussion players and instruments; the drone, too, is almost omnipresent, mostly synthesizer or sampler-generated, but also generated directly from traditional instrumentation. Musicians, instruments and genres from many locations turn up on the album – the more famous contributors being the singers Youssou N'Dour, Baaba Maal and Nusrat Fateh Ali Khan. There are also pre-existing songs and sounds, some archival, some based on Gabriel's own recordings. 'The Feeling Begins' sets the tone for the whole and is potent exercise in compositional arrangement and layering, as Gabriel set out to combine traditional elements and new technological devices and practices to create a series of evocative moods. The mood of *Passion* is surprisingly consistent. Bar a few quieter, smaller ensemble pieces, the whole follows a fairly regular pattern: drones of many colours, arrival of percussion, quietening of percussion after sequences of polyrhythmic alternation between different players and/or loops. This mood is often heavy, the steady drones connoting a stable situation and society, the other parts bringing in tensions and change, the overall effect strongly suggesting some sort of equatorial soundscape, stretching from Morocco through Northern Africa and into Central Asia – a sonic landscape that more accurately reflects the finished product than Scorsese's take on what he heard as the soundtrack part of his overall vision.

It would be easy to hear something of what Said identified as 'Orientalism' – the Westerner perceiving all other societies as part of an interesting yet basically homogenizable entity. Said did not actually say that therefore all attempts to travel, learn, live elsewhere, communicate with other peoples than your own, were necessarily suspect or doomed to fail – his point was about the use made of 'exotic knowledge' by colonial powers in the nineteenth century. As we have seen, Gabriel could be construed as a benevolent exoticist, well aware of identity as something subject to fragmentation, and in *Passion* there was a sense of blending of cultures that feasibly misrepresents their origins. I do not think that the making of the album matched the casual understanding of Orientalism – rather than taking other people's cultures and using them as decoration or titillating detail, Gabriel had assembled a supergroup of international players far more interesting than any rock combination (a parallel can perhaps be seen in Damon Albarn's collaborations in Africa, begun on *Mali Music*, 2002, and continued on *Kinshasa One*

Two, 2011, showcasing a range of Congolese musicians, and the broader Africa Express project that has seen Albarn continue to record with many African musicians). The 'exotic' sounds are at the core of the music, but the backbone is nearly always provided by Gabriel, who positions himself in the background and subsequently provides the more decorative elements around the invited musicians. The more detailed work , which is clearly designed to foreground rather than marginalize others' contributions, is in the arranging, which is the final part of the composition. Where the album itself falters, though, is in its creation of a resolutely exotic mood – to paraphrase Donald Rumsfeld, these are not unknown unknown sounds, but familiarly unfamiliar ones: 'I was trying to mix various elements, although historically inaccurate, so as to establish a living world within the film,' said Gabriel.[26] The album also insists on maintaining the same mood, which makes sense for the sake of consistency, but having taken the time to adapt the original soundtrack into the album, the sense of a unitary atmosphere based on a sort of flattened fusion bedrock of imagined sound of the Middle East has ended up as a somewhat limiting mix – musically and in terms of cultural re-presentation.

The mood is not always exactly the same, even if the scene-setting is very consistent – euphoria replaces dread, brooding or yearning, and this is signalled by the presence of vocals (for example Nusrat Fateh Ali Khan, in the track 'Passion', by far the longest on the album). The structure of the tracks follows a steady trajectory: fading in of drone, musical events, fade out. Rather than attributing this to the exigencies of making a soundtrack, maybe something else is going on. If *Passion* tries to establish a complete soundworld, based on a fusion of styles from many global locations, then its individual tracks are also microworlds, each one coming into existence and departing. Each one becomes autonomous, within a wider, more homogeneous realm. This neatly encapsulates the more material production of the work, representing the maintenance of specificities in the group's work.

The presence or otherwise of Gabriel's voice is curious: for the most part, it is very much present only as a layer, with no privilege over any others. He does not sing lyrics, although sometimes his chanting or singing approaches forms that are like series of words. There are two exceptions, where his voice comes to the forefront, and these two tracks also contain other elements that are much closer to the style of his song albums. 'A Different Drum' begins with percussion, trading rhythms across several layers. A clear synth melody takes the top line, until Youssou N'Dour's singing starts, followed by Gabriel, joining in. There is even a (wordless) chorus. 'It is Accomplished', the penultimate track, is a close cousin to 'Red Rain' from *So* and, along with 'A Different Drum', the most 'rock' of the album's 21 tracks.

Maybe it is a mistake to identify *Passion* as a world music album. But it seems to be *about* using music from around the world, creating harmony from fusion rather than absorption. The use of a Christian story as the basis for this message could be troubling, suggesting a specified dominant ideology for the 'harmony' – but I am sure Gabriel was very much interested in *The Last Temptation of Christ* as a universal story only in terms of its humanity, saying that 'normally Christ is sanitized with this halo and you don't have a sense of humanity. Scorsese was determined to portray Christ's struggle between humanity and divinity.'[27] From the liberal humanist perspective, the human is what unites, a statement that the world can, as it were, live as one.

For better or worse, *Passion* highlights the Western rock star as commissioner or patron – a role Gabriel ensures even more fully given his position as the head of the Real World studio and label, just then being launched. He said that he had conceived it as more of 'a meeting place where musicians and technologists could drop in and work together, without the barriers and hassles of the music business' – yet someone needed to be pulling the organizational and curatorial strings.[28] Real World also released *Passion: The Sources*, to highlight the music of those who worked on *Passion*. This was more than a gesture; it was a statement of political intent. It is clear that in releasing such an album, everyone's cultural capital was going to be raised, not just that of the musicians. I do not believe we should critique the attitude of all record labels through the figure of Real World, but there is a point of justifiable critique, and again, it is about the way in which music of the world is conceived, rather than a statement of facile purity about the undesirability of mixing musics. In other words, it is about one word in particular: 'sources'. The music of the world is out there to be tapped, like a well, it suggests – and maybe it is, but a source is just as easily identified as a resource, a reassuring font from elsewhere, something primordial and largely unchanging. Before going too far with this, we should also acknowledge that 'sources' of inspiration are not one-directional or straightforward, whether within or between cultures or individuals.

Gabriel himself would now take the world, its technology, its musics, its people, its political struggles, as source for music and intervention in more forthright ways, albeit mostly in music-based settings. Gabriel's music and lyrical concerns had shown a series of transitions, from the critical reappraisal of Albion, through America and into the wider world. We can also map this sequence as a move towards an increased sense of integration. It would seem, on the face of it, that critical perspectives (in Genesis), outsider perceptions and enforced marginalizations (growing from one *Peter Gabriel* album to another) gave way to a sense of the need for harmony instead of discord. This could be achieved at the level of cultural interactions: individual collaborations such as those with leading Senegalese singer Youssou N'Dour, and later with Shankar, with the Pakistani qawwali singer Nusrat Fateh Ali Khan, with Papa Wemba or Baaba Maal, and by the end of the decade many more. This also emerged from Gabriel's political (but ostensibly non-ideological) engagement and reorientation of his music. The corporate media world that his 1986 album *So* inhabited paralleled Real World's gestation, development and drive to have a public profile to sell albums, while the slow growing of *Passion* told a different story – of new modes of resistance to homogenized media and a critical nonconformity in Gabriel's oeuvre, which now occurred practically, lyrically, commercially and musically at a global level.

The humanism of *Passion*, its belief in bringing union, was one major strand of Gabriel's thinking from the 1980s onwards. It informed the business side of his activities, and his involvement in politics, particularly at this point with Amnesty, and it is there that the two parallel existences of Gabriel coincided – most clearly on the stadium concerts organized in support of Amnesty, the 'Conspiracy of Hope' tour in late 1986 and the concert in honour of Nelson Mandela's seventieth birthday held on 11 June 1988. Gabriel took a more peripheral role in the latter event, but was at the core of Amnesty's 'promotional' tour – strongly advocating not just support for the agency, but also active involvement, as a kind of entry to global citizenship, mirroring his own newly global allegiance, which included advocacy for 'Greenpeace, Amnesty, Artists Against Apartheid, Central American Peace Groups, fund-raising for the victims of Hurricane Irene'.[29] The performer, lyric narrator and musician Peter Gabriel now situated himself and his activities at the level of the world. That is the reason we cannot just ditch the term 'world music', as we can hear him holding on to the tenet that all music can work as communication, that any specific music can contribute to the evolution of any other music, and that this potential is a microcosm of the possibly utopian model of cooperation in social and geopolitical activities.

The critical edge did not go away, much as the public advocacy of human rights and support for active agencies on the one hand, and musical meetings and fusion on the other, might suggest. Instead, Gabriel's world is one that can exist only in being brought into being, in its emergence, and in distinction to the massification of capital and liberal market values. Gabriel's global is an alternative one, which in French is known as *altermondialisation* – an alternative way of globalizing. Gabriel's world is interstitially related to the one of creeping corporate homogeneity. It sometimes mirrors that one. It sometimes shares the same platforms, or makes money in very similar ways. Politically, in terms of old ideologies, it is nearly, if not quite, on the Left.

In terms of new politics, newer cultural understandings, Gabriel is involved in repositioning himself and others. This repositioning can only be thought of as dislocation – a move away from the safe context of home, changing the nature of what is 'home', the familiar, such that it is now something to be built as process in the global economy. While the world would seem to be the opposite of the domestic home, this is precisely what is interesting in the choice to identify oneself as part of the world. This 'home' carries a sense of place that is not just locational – the world, as opposed to Godalming, or New York, or Kinshasa. Place is consciously reworked by Gabriel, at all levels of his music activity, as a structure of relation, and this means that place is in flux, while also being precisely what is at stake. In other, more compromised, words, Gabriel inhabits a real world informed by his sense that it is actually a construct that is in process, structured by networks of power, some benign, others malignant. In this construct lies the possibility of change but also metamorphosis, development and interaction with what were at that point new and heightened levels of mediatization.

5 *SO* AND THE GLOBAL NETWORK

Through the 1980s, Gabriel increased his global awareness and
engagement while expanding the range of the sources for his
music. Amid this gradual development, as evidenced in the instrumentation, rhythms, collaborations and ambience of his albums
and soundtracks, came a more immediate, politically more superficial but mediatically profound encounter with the global. This
came with the international success of his 1986 album *So*, and
the many singles extracted from it, with this multimillion-selling
album making Gabriel a globally known star. This would in turn
help drive the success of his ethical and political interventions,
help the profile of his collaborators, from whichever culture they
came, and help support the Real World label, while making him a
global presence. The 1980s was a decade that saw the broadening
of the spread of Western media, particularly those of the u.s.,
in the specific shapes of the music channel MTV and the news
channel CNN. Where most artists had achieved success through
their albums and tours, commercial and sonic contact could now
be made with a much greater ease. In a way, the early 1980s was
a precursor to the Internet explosion of disseminated cultural
'product' that would occur two decades later, long after the World
Wide Web was established in 1989. The homogenizing, even
hegemonic power of English-language culture, especially that
made and/or distributed by u.s. media, was becoming apparent.
The media, whether in terms of channels, delivery devices or

what today is called 'content', contributed to the spread of a
model of global capitalism, just as they benefited from the 'freeing
up' of world markets, the growth and seeding of 'new' markets
and the ever more accessible and connected wealthier societies.

The 1980s was a decade driven by the 'free' market policies
represented by the leadership of Margaret Thatcher and Ronald
Reagan, the arrival of East and Southeast Asia in leading roles on
both supplier and consumer sides of capitalism, and the last gasp
of the 'threat' of a different social model, that is, the repressive,
supposedly communist societies living under the leadership of
the Soviet Union. As the Cold War world of mutual fear based
on massed nuclear missiles gave way to the thaw led by Soviet
premier Mikhail Gorbachev, following the rise of anti-government
forces in countries such as Poland, this was a decade that would
end with the belief that ideology, or history itself, had ended, as
exemplified by Francis Fukuyama's political philosophy best-seller
The End of History (1992), widely (mis)understood as cheerleading
for the end of socialism and the triumph of the market.[1]

While this was the wider context for *So*, and featured as the
backdrop for 'Don't Give Up', it might seem a stretch to connect
this seemingly shiny pop record, by someone who had mostly
made much more experimental work, to the decline of the
Manichean world of the Cold War. If anything, the album could
well be seen, in its slickness, its embrace of video media and a
liberal-ish politics, as a symptom of the belief in the triumph of
the superficial, the financial, the mainstream. The album and its
visual and performative avatars were far from being so naive, so
beholden to their world. *So*'s complicity with this newly neolib-
eralized world was its subject-matter, its bedrock, its ground for
self-reflection.

More than the dying Cold War and the triumph of capitalism,
the world that *So* inhabited was the particular part of globalization that was and is the cross-national media. In incorporating

some of the other 'global' interests that he had, Gabriel was able to create a complex process of mirroring, where the world of variation, difference and community was seen (and heard) enmeshed with its other, that of media access and delivery. When Marshall McLuhan offered the idea (in 1964) that the 'medium is the message', and that we should look at the delivery system of art as much as the content, he had in mind a different yet still anticipatory complexity to the one being brought into reality in the 1980s. While he coined the idea of the 'global village' as the outcome of changes of media, he could not have foreseen the later era where individual media, or media delivery systems, could themselves also constitute a meta-message for the meta-media of 'the global' or 'freedom' or 'democracy'. This is the world of *So*, a world of agonistic cultures and multilayered media (reflected in the very structure and form of the videos).

On 1 August 1981, a new channel, MTV (Music Television), began broadcasting. It did so with The Buggles's 'Video Killed the Radio Star', which was already a major international success, helmed by singer and producer Trevor Horn. The song's intelligent take on the succession of media paradigms was both right and wrong – correct in its understanding that the addition of the visual to pop songs would change expectations of what pop musicians would do, and incorrect in that we very soon had a new type of radio – just one with images as well as sounds, in the shape of MTV. In fact, Trevor Horn would continually prove, through his production work in the 1980s, that a combination of seemingly nostalgic form and practice accompanied by new technology was the way the future would now go. When MTV began, it replaced the magazine format of music programmes with endless music videos, broken up only by advertising. This breakthrough structure did not remain the format of the channel for that long. Music video historian Andrew Goodwin argues forcefully against the characterization of MTV as a one-trick, postmodernist phenomenon, and notes three phases in MTV's early life: the constant videos (to 1983), the rediscovery of programme making (1983–5), and then, from 1985 to 1987, a strong focus on metal, and the hiving off of the safer middle-of-the-road rock (MOR) or album-oriented rock (AOR) onto the channel VH1, thus creating a generational or demographic-based division of popular culture. We could add a fourth phase – one that Goodwin mentions, but not as a phase as such – which is when black music began to be adequately represented, and this came with the surge in 'gangsta rap' in the late 1980s.[2] Despite Goodwin's important observations about the very pragmatic and changeable focal points for the channel, MTV did steer the paradigm of music programming on TV, paving the way not only for television imitators but also the 'mix' format of the iPod and YouTube. Where once MTV was alone, there are now many stations (MTV itself has several), some of which offer 'reality' programmes, others concerts, sitcoms, interviews – and many that pass much of their time just showing videos for individual songs.

The commercial and artistic importance of a good video was a given by the time Gabriel was working on *So* in 1985. He had made videos previously – including the strangely minimal video for 1978's 'Modern Love', showing him dressed as a hockey player, struggling upward on a down escalator, and the video for 'Shock the Monkey', from 1982, which visually emphasized the song's lyrical interest in control. Nevertheless, it was only by the mid-1980s that Gabriel moved beyond a simple complement to the song in visual form, interspersed with shots of him singing, to a commissioned visual rendering that would more fully parallel the song. Gabriel was advanced in this respect – Michael Jackson had tested out extended narrative formats for his songs from *Thriller* (released late 1982, with the video for the title track a year later), but it was still not a widespread practice – it was not clear to record companies that videos were a wise investment. It took the colossal success of Gabriel's 'Sledgehammer', a sort of soul song by an experimental, ex-progressive rock musician, to do that. In this instance, the medium carried a commercial message that was not just about sales to the public, but the selling of an idea (the value of video) within the music 'industry'. Record companies, music channels, performers, advertisers – all began to hope to make it big on the back of visualizing the pop song, and 'Sledgehammer' remains a constant in the 'best video' charts for its detail, humour and 'show-and-tell' of the lyrics.

'Sledgehammer' was released as a single in April 1986, a harbinger of *So*, which came out in May of that year. The video drove the success of the song, which raised the awareness and sales of the album, which in turn fed the profile of the concert tour and Gabriel's public involvement with Amnesty and other organizations.[3] Gabriel's first experience of global stardom was a part of the spread of the music video as accessible art form. The critical status 'Sledgehammer''s video is accorded is due to its makers: director Stephen R. Johnson, Aardman Studios animators, including Nick Park (who would go on to make the *Wallace and Gromit* films), the Brothers Quay (influential multimedia animators) and others, which gave it an instant kudos, although these artists were not so widely known at the time. The combination of artistic and production values were perhaps part of the reason for the video's popularity, and were certainly behind the granting to it of multiple awards in 1987. What is curious is not just the fate of this video in becoming a figurehead for the globalization of cultural media, but that it was effectively a video that launched an album. A music video would no longer be a reflection or a secondary supplement, but a condensation of, or a spoiler for, the whole.

Gabriel acknowledged the artistic value of music video in the commercial format of a VHS cassette (and LaserDisc) of videos of the songs of the album, entitled *cv*. The music would no longer be encased in one medium; instead, new technologies, formats and media were altering the shape of pop music, and Gabriel's venture into pop coincided entirely with this change, signalling that he was aware that the domain of experimentation did not need to remain constrained within the songs, but could stretch even beyond performance into other modes of presentation of the material.

> I'm probably a sort of natural ham. I've always liked multi-media things. I think the end of the eighties and nineties will see a second multi-media phase, as we get standard TV images, film images, 3-D, holophonic sound, all this stuff. I think people will demand visuals as a result of MTV and the video explosion.[4]

This emerging techno-aesthetic is something that informed Gabriel's work from that point on, more so than most mainstream musicians.

'Sledgehammer' combined multiple animation techniques, but most memorably, it used stop-motion and plasticine. Plasticine copies were made of Gabriel, of objects, buildings and, yes, sledgehammers. These were then merged with actual filmed footage, building a frame at a time. The video used these materials and techniques to represent the lyrics in very literal fashion, so to some extent actually obfuscating the sexual subtext. The music is dominated by Gabriel's Otis Redding referencing, in the form of wind instruments that sought to replicate the sound of 1960s R&B, but also in the shape of Wayne Jackson, part of The Memphis Horns, someone who had played with Otis Redding and who had helped define the sound of Stax Records through being in the label's house band.[5] These explicit reference points remind us that America manifests as a driving force behind contemporary culture throughout Gabriel's oeuvre, and with *So* there were several key elements of the music, and of the lyrics, that made this explicit.

Beyond this, the media dissemination of the songs was what made *So* a core part of MTV's globalizing music mission.

There is plenty to read in the video of 'Sledgehammer' from its surrealistic approach (in song and video elements).[6] Commentators all seem to accept Gabriel's authorial representation of the song as being about sex. The song is indeed a pastiche of the Stax romantic song which was essentially all about sex, in its lyrics and in the pulsing beat and horn combination. But how far is this actually the case when the material is examined closely? We know that Gabriel also participated heavily in the planning stages of the video, and other than the sperm shot and coursing blood indicating new life or the building of excitement, all the 'sex metaphors' are presented exactly, in visual literalism, thus exaggerating the double entendre aspect of the song, as opposed to making it less metaphorical. Readers and viewers can be too hasty to attribute a definitive meaning to a song, particularly when reiterating statements made by the lyric writer. Instead, I think we might wish to look more closely at what is actually being said and shown.

Let's begin with the object 'sledgehammer' – purportedly indicating the thrusting desire of male sexual conquest. The critic Brenda Schmahmann muses that this might not be so straightforward, but quickly covers over this threatening uncertainty with the idea that if Gabriel (as shown in the video) pounds himself, then it is about masturbation. Well, maybe. But does the sledgehammer itself have 'obviously phallic connotations'?[7] It does not act when upright; it acts when made to descend. It weighs downward, not up, and instead of controlling or entering anything, it hammers – that is, it hits, flatly, not phallicly. If you believe that all aggression or use of tools is inherently (or 'symbolically') masculine, then perhaps this argument still works, but it is still not clear (or even suggestively unclear) what the sexual part of the lyric 'let me be your sledgehammer' is. I suppose that incessant, steady hammering might lead to some sort of pleasure, but wouldn't the rhythm ('been feeding the rhythm') be better in this scenario if more mechanically based, and less about lifting, dropping, hammering from a long way away to maximize force?

The 'I' that desires to be the sledgehammer is not depicted as a virile tool-wielder. Instead, the figure of the triumphant performer that had so quickly become a staple of video representation is made much more complex and less of a subject, let alone a dominant humper. For all the cheery expression and jaunty moves of the participating Gabriel, he becomes a character in someone else's piece, and actually what categorizes animated Gabriel is his becoming-object.[8] He does not so much pound himself as fall into a world of object relations far outside his control. The rhythm he feels is one that takes over the body, the rhythm of sexual heat maybe, but, at the risk of labouring the point, one of the wall-crunching, cavity-opening tool suggested by the title.

Gabriel is shown as a set of partial objects when first seen, parts of his head shown in isolation, undoing his subject identity. From then on, whether in stop-motion or plasticine claymation, he is assailed by object after object, and accepts this with cheery fatalism. Not only is his face partial, his body subject to attack, but the stop-motion removes the continuity that adds up to subject agency. The strangeness of the uncanny proximity to the singer singing a song while being fragmented spatially and into micro-slices of time takes the prospect of tool mastery even further from reach.

As the video progresses, it illustrates directly the references to nouns and actions indicated in the lyrics (these are then reiterated by Gabriel in live performance settings). Many of these are to do with transport – steam train, aeroplane, big dipper, bumper car. Others are to nature – fish, vegetation, fruit – and all act on Gabriel's jerkily moving features, sometimes

Still from the 'Sledgehammer' music video, directed by Stephen R. Johnson, with animation by the Brothers Quay and Aardman Animations.

surrounding, other times engulfing or displacing. So at one of the rare times when we hear a double entendre, 'show me round your fruitcage, I will be your honeybee', we are taken far from the vagina, as a load of fruit first frames Gabriel's face and then supplants it as he sings the relevant line. Gabriel's head is also encased in glass or ice, then smashed clear; a sort of avant-garde shed is built around or on it; at still another point, it is painted blue, doused, occupied by fish; and claymation Gabriel has his head opened, turned into a blue, singing stick-creature, and merged with artworks.

Finally, the closing section sees a more complete Gabriel dancing around, again in stop-motion, with the responding chorus of female singers, then with furniture and piles of objects, and also with a mass of people. A tired Gabriel aims for sleep in his

Two stills from the 'Sledgehammer' music video. It made startling use of claymation and stop-motion animation; Gabriel was required to lie under a sheet of glass for sixteen hours while the video was shot.

chair and ends up referencing the BBC's *Old Grey Whistle Test* credit sequence, by replicating the dancing figure from those credits – made of sparse lights over a black suit on a dark background – and leaves the building, much as that music magazine programme would do in the face of newer approaches from MTV and its imitators.[9]

I think something else is going on in 'Sledgehammer' beyond being a song about sex. The video, lyrics and music heighten each other and take it and the listener/viewer outside the realm of straighforward sex, whether parodic or potentially misogynistic, and into the domain of the more radically erotic. As we have seen with his work in Genesis, that connection is entirely likely, but we need to bring out the detail. In fact, what 'Sledgehammer', taken as audiovisual device, does is partake of the death-bound strangeness of the surrealist philosopher-pornographer Georges Bataille's eroticism, which is 'the deliberate loss of self'.[10] The interplay of sex, music, subject, object, with the attacked Gabriel, clay Gabriel, hammering and self-hammering Gabriel, is about transformation, about becoming something other, including becoming erotic. The whole video, and the song's relentless placement of object metamorphoses through (or as) intimate engagement, brings 'Sledgehammer' to a place of perpetual mutation, and also endless repetition (beat, chorus, trumpet, MTV showing it over and over). Sex is just one part of endless becoming, and the hammer smashes the veneer of solid existence (clay Gabriel bashes and forcibly remoulds his head with hammer hands). Curiously, then, Gabriel was still addressing alienation, strange drives, separation as well as togetherness, in a song and video of continual movement *towards*.

This approaching, this move towards something, echoed Gabriel's turn towards world music and to global politics that grew through the 1980s. 'Sledgehammer' introduced the album to the world, and it also heralded Gabriel's definitive move to using advancing media to extend the meaning of his songs and performance. In so doing, he was at the forefront of the avant-garde utilization of the format of video, making it a form that could reflect upon itself, and advance experimentally, where the majority of video making was basically a set of moving photographs of performing singers and bands – or more accurately, performers miming their songs. Gabriel would of course do this, but his collaborative use of media would ensure the undermining of the centrality of performer as star.

In 1987 Gabriel released the video collection *cv*, comprising the singles from *So*, including two versions of 'Don't Give Up' and a video for the non-single track 'Mercy Street', thus cementing the idea of a video album. In fact, this format idea was never widely used – certainly not outside the more industrial and experimental metal genres, with the recent honourable exceptions of Beyoncé's *Beyoncé* (2013) and *Lemonade* (2016) and Frank Ocean's *Endless* (2016), although these releases act more as a resistance to the perma-visualization of pop that is YouTube. The album of *So* was not a fixed object, as, in addition to the video complement, the vinyl edition was made up of eight tracks, missing the collaboration with Laurie Anderson, 'This is the Picture (Excellent Birds)', which featured on cassette and CD. Later it would transpire that Gabriel had never liked the sequencing of the album, which had been determined by the compromise reached between Gabriel and his record company that sought to maximize bass on particular tracks in the vinyl format. Since 2012's remaster, *So* contains the nine tracks, in an ur-sequence approved by Gabriel, and even appears on vinyl in that form, inside the 25th Anniversary box version of the album.

So offered connections between tracks rather than an overarching theme, although, as I am suggesting in this chapter, the album contained the meta-theme of globalizing neoliberalism and media. This is prominent in 'Big Time', a song nearly as jaunty as 'Sledgehammer' and with a similar soul feel, using the same horn section, the same backing singers and a similar video, directed by the same director. Like 'Sledgehammer', this song contains more complexity than initially appears the case (conversely, the more complex content of 'Mercy Street' is more transparent). 'Big Time' is told by a narrator who is 'on my way, I'm making it', and as the song progresses, he leaves his small town and 'small ideas' behind, to become part of the 'big time', and success awaits. The track is subtitled 'suc cess', and, reading the gap as meaningful, we can see that Gabriel is referring to the sucking of 'cess' – that is, of waste – and so to succeed is to eat shit. So more is going on behind the scenes, and Gabriel uses the track's apparent cheerleading for neoliberal ideas of realizing yourself through fame and finance to filter through a critique of that same attitude. Writing of the song in 2012, he said:

> at home I liked to bury myself in normal family life in the English countryside, but I could also enjoy being a popstar out on the town in New York. So the song was a reflection on America and the UK in the 1980s but also there was a bit of self-mockery in there.[11]

The sneering at the 'smallness' he leaves behind, and the embrace of 'bigness', so much so that he cannot stop, paints the narrator as someone lost in the very process of seemingly 'making it'. His head expands, and not just through the usual metaphor of thinking oneself to be great: the protagonist's head really does expand, necessitating a mountainous bed and soft pillow to attempt to bolster it. In the closing call-and-response section, Gabriel lists all the things – objects, wealth, body parts – that are expanding. He pushes the logic of these metaphors into something more sur-real, to speculate on what would happen if you actually kept expanding, and all of your things grew for ever, in the 'big time'.

This surrealist strategy takes the song beyond a simple critique of the desire for betterment through attainment in a market economy to make it more of a moral fable – be careful what you wish for; what if everything really did expand? The end of the song is ambiguous, ending on a repeated 'big' after talking of his 'bulge' (presumably either money or an erection). Expansion goes on for ever, the narrator moves on to a scale that is outside everything else.

Gabriel's take on the society of acquisition is one of scale, of continual scale change, such that an individual is called on to be restive instead of resting. The ultimate outcome is the loss of self in bigness. Time itself becomes 'big', difficult to fill, other than through more expansion, and in this, Gabriel's hapful narrator resembles Ubu, the creation of proto-surrealist Alfred Jarry. Gabriel used this absurd perspective to develop the wider perspective in 'Big Time', the metanarrative of the complete global economic structure that was building in the 1980s, a vacuous and pernicious call to perpetual growth.

If 'Big Time' aims big, 'Don't Give Up' uses a more intimate setting to address the economic failings of unfettered capitalism. Gabriel took the images of Depression-era u.s. by Dorothea Lange as a surrogate set of images for the dismal effects of the 'restructuring' of the British economy in the decade: 'the reference to the great depression of America in the 1930s was to draw attention to mass unemployment in the uk in the mid-80s.'[12] 'Don't Give Up', though, personalized this context, drawing it inward to the tale of a couple in dialogue, with Gabriel recounting the state of the economy and how he felt his place in the world slipping, or being taken, away. Kate Bush supplied a more positive voice in the choruses. Bush was perhaps cast in a traditional female role here, reassuring the anxious male who is supposed to put bread on the table but cannot, but she also represented the changing face of the workplace – nowhere in the song does she talk as a wife who waits for the man to return from (job) hunting. Nowhere does he apologize directly to her for his failure. So what we also have here is a highly effective comment on the reduction of the traditionally male-occupied parts of the Western economy.

Kate Bush's character represented the future, not just of a change in which certain sectors of the economy were to be prioritized, but also a recognition that future working would be more social, service- and/or community-based. The simple video, directed by Kevin Godley and Lol Creme (both previously of 10cc, and successful as a music duo as well as being video directors), does, however, suggest the two voices of the song are joined together, as the two singers are physically entwined, turning towards the camera as they take their turn for their vocal contributions. This is, no doubt, largely what Gabriel intended (once Kate Bush was on board), but as with 'Big Time', 'Don't Give Up' extends its comments into the wider realm, and in this case the reassurance offered by Bush is the holding open of utopia, of prospects beyond the current failing and exclusion. Its music is much more meditative, slow-paced, 'more from a roots tradition of American folk and spiritual music', as Gabriel said, and the presence of a coda, with restatements of the title, suggests hope for the narrators as well as more widely.[13] Instead of the 'big time', a wider or longer view would be needed so as not to give way to despair.

The prospect of hope, the psychology of adjustment, along with falling outside supposed norms, continues in 'Mercy Street', one of a set of three tracks that overtly addresses a range of institutional responses to human cognitive and affective responses. 'Mercy Street', 'That Voice Again' and 'We Do What We're Told (Milgram's 37)' address the location of individual subjectivity in relation to others, to society and to expected behaviours, as well as looking at those questions through the prism of professional psychoanalysis. Where earlier Gabriel albums had mused on internal states of mind, often found in the hinterlands of the social, on *So* the self is in the process of relocating as an outward-facing entity, responding in different ways to focused self-reflection. 'Mercy Street' was dedicated to the confessional poet Anne Sexton, who began writing poetry as a sort of treatment for psychological problems, originally suggested to her by a psychiatrist. Sexton killed herself in 1974, after producing a substantial body of writing, including the play *45 Mercy Street* and what would be a posthumously published collection under that name; it is clear that as a figure of hope, the meaning she represented was a complex one. Nonetheless, amid despair and disconnection from the world, Sexton's work was reaching for connection, for some sort of redemption. Gabriel's song takes inspiration from Sexton's life, her creativity and mental struggle, and also her imagistic style, adapting these into a more general set of ideas and tableaux that, while drawing on Sexton, do not look for the affirmation of reader recognition in order to achieve their effect. Gabriel's voice is quiet, suggesting not only empathy for the subject of the song, but also that the listener receive this empathy as a way in to the character.[14] It also signals a mood that is far from unique to Sexton's biographical situation, and not limited to Gabriel's strong impression of it.[15]

Gabriel's 'Mercy Street' makes oblique reference to how Sexton conjures images of hopeful contact, with a very strong sense that the way in which the female character in the song receives assistance is far from benign. The verses see the character engaging in small actions, reflecting on what she encounters as the outside (verse one), in various insides (verses two and three), and dreaming of her father in a boat, a boat that intersperses song and video alike, arrestingly suggesting a kind of Charon-like figure in the form of the father, taking Anne to her death, but also to her ease. Leading music video critic Carol Vernallis argues that the 'verses are oriented toward the individual, the

intimate, the secret and the illicit; those in the chorus explore
personal relations and provide the narrative'.[16] The first verse sees
the female character explicitly reflecting streets, buildings and
the interactions of others, apart from her; the second also brings
a visualization of outside inward. In the interim, verses one and
two are split by a chorus, or something like an 'inter-verse', that is
not going to be repeated, even if its image of the boat in darkness
is. Verse three sees the character exploring interiors: drawers, a
Christian confessional box, a more medical institution. Exploring
might be the wrong word, but not entirely, as the confessional and
psychiatric institution both exist in order to invite self-reflection
and discovery. If the priest in the song is also a doctor, who 'can
handle the shocks', we are talking about deeply oppressive treat-
ments at the hands of predominantly male institutions, that is, in
electroconvulsive therapy (ECT). The 'darkness' she discovers is not
just an inevitable part of her, but is fed by the institutional interest
in and manipulation of the 'interior', whether of their buildings,
drawers, or physical and mental inner space. This representative
of repressive confessionals recalls and recasts 'The Supernatural
Anaesthetist' and the 'doktor' of 'The Colony of Slippermen' on
The Lamb Lies Down on Broadway, both of whom aimed to attack
their 'patients' through remoulding or killing them. The encounter
with these two on *Lamb* precedes Rael's re-emergence into the city,
but in 'Mercy Street' the escape that beckons is the open sea, an
emptiness overseen by the ambiguous figure of Anne's father.

The same figure is a key part of the 'relation-based' choruses,
as the narrator will dream of 'Mercy Street' 'in your daddy's
arms'. Outside of the sheltering yet maybe too close and too
deadly father, we should also note that the perspective of the song
has changed: from hovering like a camera eye, the narrator moves
in to talk, as if from inside her dreams, to Anne Sexton. Even
more interesting is the punning line 'wear your inside out', which
indicates the outwardness and connectedness hoped for as mercy,

but also the fatigue of existing in darkness, and making light of it, either through interactions, through writing or, in the song itself, going out on the boat, never to return. The outward and inward motions of chorus and verse respectively are very little mirrored in the music, which remains steady, though the instrumental part becomes more forceful towards, if not at, the end.

The celebration of Sexton and indictment of 'care' institutions evident in the lyrics follows on, on the new ordering of *So*, from 'That Voice Again', a far more upbeat assessment of the mind and behaviour-focused professions. This song is about the narrator's own hope, mostly understood to reflect a moment in his therapeutic and emotional history that is not entirely positive, as it charts the struggle between a wish for and a rejection of completion through living with the addressee, the 'you' of the song. The voice that the narrator hears is ostensibly an internal voice that expresses the fear of openness and connection to an other. It strikes me that this voice could be something much more actively troublesome, suggesting other avenues for pleasure and fulfilment, or even the therapeutic voice itself, as an unwitting barrier to authentic relationship-making. The 'voice' could be the one of self-awareness, the one heard by the 37 per cent of volunteers in Stanley Milgram's authority experiment who said no to punishing others in his controversial test in which volunteers were invited to administer an electric shock to other volunteers (actually actors) if they got answers to questions wrong. The track 'We Do What We're Told (Milgram's 37)', originally devised in 1981 and a regular part of the 1982 tour set list, is a distillation of Milgram's discovery of the unquestioned acceptance of authority by the majority of people.

Some of the controversy around the experiment related to the ethics of exploiting and/or fooling participants, but also its framing as a formally sanctioned university experiment (it was conducted for the first time at Yale University), which could be considered a potentially distorting factor if we were to want to find out for real how many people would hurt others on the basis of being told to do so. In any case, Gabriel was fascinated by the study, and in the song's earlier incarnation used it in parodic form, getting the audience to repeat the line 'We Do What We're Told' over and over. As he says, 'I think some people got the irony, but not everyone.'[17] Other than that glimpse of an analytical reading of the experiment, Gabriel was not using the track as a critique of the psychological establishment, but instead to gnaw at the worry that individuals have internalized authority to such an extent that any real power that wishes to exploit this will be able to.

On the new ordering of *So*, 'This is the Picture (Excellent Birds)' extends the lab meditation of 'We Do What We're Told'. Written and performed with Laurie Anderson, this track was devised in response to a commission from the pioneering video and sound artist Nam June Paik. Like 'Mercy Street', this song has a video even though it was not slated for release as a single. The experimental content and form of the previous track continues in a musing on mediatized experience in a way that strangely pre-empts the success of Gabriel's own imminent video-mediatization, and is a direct enactment of Anderson's musing that Gabriel was always thinking about 'how else you could experience music'.[18]

The album (as now configured) ends by heading outwards, with 'In Your Eyes', a highly positive love song directed at the loved one and expressing how all the narrator's conscious thought and self-awareness fall away in their presence. His will to autonomous freedom is sacrificed so he 'can reach out from the inside'. On the original 1986 release this song bridged 'That Voice Again' and 'Mercy Street', and for all that that running order was a pragmatic one based on heightening the bass of 'In Your Eyes', the run of three songs did create its own dynamic, of rising and then falling away, even if with warmth in 'Mercy Street'. A triumphant, utopian track, 'In Your Eyes' brings the other close, as a guide, inspiration, presence. The outwardness of *So* is psychological, partially political, but also gender-based: women had never been so present on Gabriel's albums, and here were female collaborators, subjects of songs and lyrical addressees. Without being in any way a feminist album, it is as if Gabriel was moving from a fully male interior into an external world made up of more than just men (even if the main vocal partner on the track itself is Youssou N'Dour).

Musically, the presence of non-rock instrumentation and musicians was clear, if not overstated. Far from being a resource to be exploited, 'world music' acted as a way of altering Gabriel's own direction, and when that seems to benefit from a particular presence of person or sound, it was used, as *normal*, not as an exotic embellishment, just as Gabriel was doing with non-Western musicians and sounds on his soundtracks. For example, the Brazilian percussion on 'Mercy Street' is there not for colour, but to estrange the lyrical content and illustrate that the concern raised by one woman is something that extends across human cultures. A more valid point for criticism might be that N'Dour's contribution to the fade-out chorus of 'In Your Eyes' is very fleeting. However, this vocal contribution was recorded first. The song was meant to close the album, as it now does, indicating the outward direction of Gabriel's music (also audible in having multiple other voices at the conclusion, dominated by N'Dour). The brevity of this contribution would be rectified in the dramatically extended version of the song on the upcoming tours, where N'Dour had a significant part in Gabriel's set and as support act.

So was not just an album (and as noted, as an album its definitive structure remained open) but also the set of videos that accompanied and expanded it, taking the commercially released form of the *cv* videocassette. At the time, rock and pop artists were beginning to see videos as saleable commodities and art-works in their own right, as opposed to being merely promotional tools, and so were put on sale directly, often across a range of competing formats. The prices, like those of CDs, were based on the never-discussed notion that a video release was like a vinyl album, only better, either through the addition of images or enhanced fidelity (a farcical claim for first-generation CDs), and so the prices were higher, without the extra material that the formats could already have permitted. The 'war' of multiple competing formats never resulted in a significant price drop. Gabriel's *cv* was not a bad offender, since it included different versions of songs and videos that would not be shown on TV as they did not exist as mere promos.

In hindsight, the use of new formats for recording seems like a key moment in the changing patterns of commercial music releases and their consumption, but concerts too were in an era of redevelopment. Gabriel himself came to embrace a more expansive performance than at any time since the 1975 *Lamb* tour (and would expand this dramatically on later tours). The album's success also meant that Gabriel's inclusion on multi-performer bills served as a recognition of his political engagement, and those would benefit in turn from his commercial power. Amnesty International continued the boom in mass stadium charity events with the 'Conspiracy of Hope' tour (1986), on which Gabriel featured prominently. This tour would be followed by a massive world tour in support of the *So* album. With Amnesty, Gabriel began to knit together the threads of his diversifying political and musical involvement, contacts and direction. The massive sales of *So* and the global recognition that came through the highly advanced set of videos for the album meant that he had more capacity to promote 'world music'. With *So*, Gabriel began to merge two competing models of the global: the first being the awareness of a world, musical and political, beyond the West, and

Peter Gabriel performs on stage with Youssou N'Dour during Gabriel's 'This Way Up' tour, Ahoy, Rotterdam, 8 September 1987.

within which individuals could and should do more than passively criticize; the second was the beginning of the contemporary wave of globalization, almost in anticipation of the connectivity of the Internet and its creation of at least virtual mobility. Gabriel's outward-looking perspective of the 1980s began to encompass the media, in the throes of mass expansion. It was still the case that in order to inhabit or move about in that newly mediatized world, older forms of new media, such as electronics, planes and roads, would come into play for the 'This Way Up' tour which promoted and further enhanced *So*.

Gabriel's solo concerts up to this point had eschewed stadium dynamics in favour of an anti-performance style that drew attention to those very expectations in minimizing them. The same drive persisted in the 'This Way Up' tour, which started in Canada and the USA in 1986, ending in the officially recorded Athens concerts in late 1987, but also saw Gabriel beginning to use newer technologies, paving the way for subsequently more theatrical outings.[19] The 1986–7 tour featured a lot of choreographed moves, particularly between Gabriel, David Rhodes and Tony Levin, which added an element of showmanship but also deflated the stadium rock expectations of dominant masculine rock skills, as they instead embraced self-parody and purposely trite dance moves in line with the lateral group shuffle of easy listening combo The Shadows. The careful staging of movement aided the filming of the show, and while some of Gabriel's exaggerated hand and bodily moves (like marching in 'Solsbury Hill') play to the live audience, the interplay of performers seems at least as much visually conceived for large-screen viewing. The concert film featured initially on the video release *PoV*, released in 1991, framed by other documentary tour footage. The complete show, directed by Michael Chapman and produced by Martin Scorsese, appeared more recently as *Live in Athens* as part of the 25th Anniversary box set of *So*. Despite the tardiness of the eventual release of the complete filmed version, the process of filming and the effect this introduced to the concert were part of Gabriel's move to integrate new approaches to the concert format, in tandem with his own performance. It is worth noting that this attention to media, technology and to moving the spotlight onto and away from the singer was occurring at a time when stadium rock was no longer the privilege of a few major stars, but an increasingly regular mode of doing concerts, particularly as it would allow bands to play a small number of massive concerts per country. Gabriel was part of this stadium rock moment, yet consciously incorporated it as an element to be played with, rather than just leaving it as an unspoken 'natural' mass phenomenon.

The peak of both his performance and that of the technology is in the sequence of 'No Self Control' and 'Mercy Street'. The former ends with Gabriel rolling on the stage, trying to evade the descending, attacking gantries that on other occasions highlight Gabriel in spotlights. The gantries tie in with the lyrical focus of a mind under attack, which leads a person (in the song) to turn physically on the bodies of others. As the lights sweep low over him, he stays either prone or in kneeling position throughout 'Mercy Street', and the song ends with him lying on the floor. As Gabriel represents the character, and/or the poet Anne Sexton herself, he is embraced by the slowly moving lights, sheltered by colour. This part illustrates the search for tranquillity, but not being able to rise up reflects the part of the song that is about institutional control and the limits to how far the institution can countenance complete release through treatment, as it maintains a feeling of being trapped by fear and abuse. This sense of being entrapped within a supposedly nurturing environment is heightened by Gabriel screaming on the stage floor, leading into the closing short verse about the boat and the sea that points to death, but also, to some extent, calmness. Gabriel thereby exaggerates and incorporates yet another variant on psychological help, in the form of expressive therapies supposed to allow catharsis. Here, the catharsis happens only when the screaming can stop, and the sea offers some sort of relief.

Elsewhere, much of the performance was not too different from any large-scale concert, but in terms of the progression of his concert style, we can see two important developments. First, there was the increasingly portable technology, in fact most

prominent in the opening 'This is the Picture', where the five
musicians played wireless keyboards and guitars, and Gabriel sang
through a headset microphone (used by him throughout, and by
all of the members of the band at points, even if only briefly).
Gabriel and David Sancious were also using samplers onstage, in
what some would have considered problematic in terms of the
expected delivery of instrumental skill by stadium rock bands.

The appearance of Youssou N'Dour is much more substantial
in the live setting, making the point forcefully that 'world music'
can integrate with rock music, with his band Super Étoile de
Dakar opening the show, and featuring in the encore tracks of 'In
Your Eyes' and 'Biko'. The combination of songs resulted from
not only a choice of two separate moods, but an attempt to move
beyond the possible Western conception of Africa as a place in
need of liberal guilt or pity, and the expansion of 'In Your Eyes'
signals the vital force of fusion music that long pre-dated external
'discoveries' of it. The song is very much a vocal duet, with the
band doubled in size, and most of them getting to join in with
the dancing that time has not improved. Gabriel would develop a
better sense of how to punctuate rock with dance moves in later
tours, but here his ethnic embroidery-topped moves are awkward
to behold.

On the other hand, if we can get over the over-elaborated
fun of the dancing, there is the political point about integrating
musicians and musics, and also a playful side being developed
beyond Gabriel's own acting or solo moves that further removes
the concert from rock earnestness. Mention should be made of
the 'stage dive', which Gabriel had been drawn to ever since 1970,
brought in this case to a fine point of realization. In fact, as he falls
slowly back into the crowd to be carried aloft in 'Lay Your Hands
on Me', the stage dive / crowdsurfing retains the capacity to mock
the power of the stage performer that it had on the previous tour,
but here it feels much more celebratory, and Gabriel is utterly

adrenalized as he is heaved back onstage by the minders. In the context of *So*'s lyrical concerns and Gabriel's outward-locatedness, it further diminishes the capacity for isolation (whereas before it was more about reducing 'ego'). Where once the stage dive was submitted to by Gabriel as a staging point between various pathological outlooks, the lighter approach of this tour shows an offering of self strongly echoed in several of the tracks of *So*. From here it would be several years to the next album, *Us*, but *So* marks an outward psychological path, an upward commercial rise, and the beginnings of immersion in a digitalizing global culture, in parallel to his immersion in the 'world' that came into media focus through the decade.

Peter Gabriel crowdsurfing during the 1987 concert filmed and released as *Live in Athens*.

6 ALL OF US

Even as Gabriel toured some of the world with his 'This Way Up' tour, following the global success of *So* and with his burgeoning profile as a politically engaged artist, it was still possible to imagine 'the world' as other, as something beyond and bigger than anyone could access from one position. In philosophy, writers have referred to the world as the object or set of objects within which, on which, or against which humans move. Others have suggested that there is no real world, or that we could never know it, or that it is real but somewhere else, perhaps withdrawn from our grasp. In practical terms, very few could conceive of a world that was entirely familiar, or capable of being brought close, made homely. *So* and the mediatization of his album through artist-made video constructed Gabriel as a global figure. This happened in parallel to his role as a spokesperson for Amnesty International, and his continued political engagement, which had begun with his powerful anthem publicizing the South African state's murder of Stephen Biko. The tours of the late 1980s saw Gabriel presenting visual and stage performances on a large scale, in combination with a much more serious element of political commentary, such that the latter could pass by subliminally. Sometimes it was much more direct, but still used sparingly, and always a performative assertion of what was most important, such as ending concerts with 'Biko' and closing it with the statement 'the rest is up to you.'

The twin globalizing imperatives of activism and playing the hits from *So* were complemented by a different enterprise, in the shape of Real World – studio, record label and developer of concerts of 'world music'. Perversely, perhaps, this set of projects represented a re-localization of Gabriel, even as his sphere of activity and influence became that of the global. The Real World studio, established in Box in southwest England, is in a set of reconfigured buildings that begs to be described as 'nestling' in its surroundings of river and green fields (and also slightly sonically intrusive railway line), and close to where Gabriel has lived for many years. The studios are less than 5 miles from Solsbury Hill, so at the heart of the global mission lies this return 'home', a home that was never an actual home or birthplace to Gabriel, so somewhat unusual in being a decentred place of origin, a kind of dissonant familiarity.

In 1989 Gabriel released *Passion*, his album based on the soundtrack of *The Last Temptation of Christ*, with the catalogue number RW1. At the same time, Real World also brought out albums by Tabu Ley Seigneur Rochereau (from Zaire), Orquesta Revé (from Cuba), the Musicians of the Nile (Egypt), and the collection curated by Gabriel, mentioned earlier, entitled *Passion: The Sources*. From this early seed would grow a collection, spanning the entire world and many different cultures, that would chart a conscious path between traditional and new music styles, with very different cultural affiliations (national, local, class, migratory, religious, secular, radical or conservative in its original setting, professional, cadre-based or autonomous in its making). Real World was not an anthropological project, a patronizing ethno-sourcing, but an attempt to build a broad picture of music of the current moment, one that looked outside existing structures of popular music distribution in order to bring musicians into that very world.

The world of 1989 was still not the globalized world we all inhabit today, albeit at different bitrates and with very different

experiences of the outcomes of global economic activity. The
first optic fibre laid that was capable of dramatically raising
communication speed was anchored into place only in 1988, and
the protocols of the World Wide Web were developed by Tim
Berners-Lee in 1989. In practice, the Internet was still several
years away for most non-institutional users. The Internet did not
bring about globalization, and neither would it be true to state
that only the contemporary period has witnessed globalization.
But we can say that the developing interconnectedness in place in
the 1980s created the conditions for the Internet to work as a proto-
global entity and began to mould the sense of world-dwelling
through communicational connectedness. The termination of
the Soviet bloc meant that the idea of a First and Second world,
of capitalism and communism respectively, disappeared, often to
the accompaniment of gloating from right-wingers (on the back
of their own destructive putsch within Western capitalism that
took place in the 1980s, in the form of financial market deregu-
lation). In theory, the non-aligned 'Third World' could now join
'the' world. The term 'Third World' was initially designed to
describe regimes outside of the two opposing realms of capitalism and so-called communism, but would ultimately take on the
mantle of the umbrella term for the disadvantaged nations of the
world. Clearly the globalization of 'one world' would be a long
way off, and when it came, it would cement a hierarchy already
in place.

The notion of world music represented an idealized way of
thinking about the entry of previously non-aligned musics into the
world of the 'music industry'. 'World music' could be a standard-
bearer for harmonious cohabitation. Largely, as we now know, it
became a synonym for valorizing locality and authenticity while
also associating all these local authentic musics as part of one
category, easily digestible as 'that' music from somewhere else.
I think when we look at Real World's mission, and the way that

it is exemplified on *Passion: Sources*, we can start to think beyond the 'world music: good or bad' discussion, which shows no sign of abating in the professionalized debate among Western writers about what everyone else's music should be called, or how it should be represented.

Real World started out by expanding on the work of WOMAD, giving it a firmer basis, and operating what we would now call vertical integration – a business that operated every part, every level, of the process. Real World would commission, compile and invite artists to record and/or release. Artists would use the Real World studios, then the company would oversee the release all the way to distribution. In encouraging world music, Real World could tap into Gabriel's global vision, where all music was seen as having a shared source or undercurrent, along with its own distinctive elements, and this pragmatic linkage would represent an ethical commitment, mirroring his other, more political interventions. On the liner notes for *Passion: Sources*, he writes of WOMAD as an outlet for 'pure enthusiasm for world music' and clarifies that Real World represents a deepening of that commitment. The outlook of Real World is interesting in its view of the 'world' of world music. It is clear that the long-standing debates around the term and its commercial mobilization have yielded a greater self-awareness, compared to earlier discourses of simply uniting musics from across the world, bringing them together in some amorphous way. Real World states that the company 'releases recordings of superb musicians from all over the world', and although what it promotes could be thought of as world music, the mission states that 'the reality of the Real World output extends beyond this categorization' and that the origin of the musicians is irrelevant ('irrespective of the nationality of artists creating it').[1] This is a very useful and critical perspective. Real World is aware of the over-valorizing of the roots of musicians identified as part of world music, and challenges the orthodoxy that what is interesting about 'exotic' sounds is not the music but the geographical branding. Real World aims instead for a united world where Gabriel's globally networked sound (first heard in 'The Rhythm of the Heat') operates as a kind of unifying essence, a Platonic music, underlying all potential specific manifestations.

Alternatively, we could conceive of all the music produced as being but phenotypical expressions of the genotype – variations on an underlying, shared DNA. This is not the same as saying that only the music counts – it is an explicit statement of liberal universalism that fundamentally all humanity has a shared essence that then expresses itself differently in and as culture. Real World insists strongly on not fetishizing the specific origins of its contributors – as musicians can be brought together regardless of any already shared cultural inheritance. Critics might point to this position as the ultimate wiping out of distinctive identity, and therefore an elision of material realities in favour of an easily digestible cultural product, but in fact these are very much part of the musical presentation: Real World as a label has a strongly didactic outlook, but musicians are not chosen on the basis of a curious national or ethnic belonging. In the face of globalizing music in the form of heavily mediatized international stars, Real World does valorize a sort of authenticity, something akin to 'roots' music's claims to being the 'real stuff', but it does so without privileging the 'traditional' over the contemporary.

The mixing of musics is at the core of the possibility of some sort of genuine world music. Real World has served as a regular channel for collaborations between musicians who may otherwise never have met – sometimes highly purposefully, as in the label's Recording Week in 1991, which brought together huge numbers of musicians from around the world to play together, and also on the collaborative album *Big Blue Ball* (2008), documenting multifarious recombinations of musicians through the 1990s and 2000s. From the beginning, and nowhere more clearly than on

Gabriel's own *Passion* and his curated *Passion: Sources*, the interest
has been in hybrid forms. The idea of any particular music being
entirely hermetic, free of cross-cultural, transhistorical reference
was rejected from the start. This is the great boon of starting from
a liberal humanist position – the assumption of unity is not about
sameness but about connectedness. It is clear that for Gabriel
and Real World, music is about reconnecting – sometimes to the
world, sometimes to others – but more profoundly, music itself
is not just a source but a vector of connection. Connection may
imply interfering with or diminishing established, supposedly
enclosed entities, but Gabriel has used conscious hybridization as
a way of revealing the always already hybrid nature of any music
from a particular location. He has done this in his music (heavily
inflected by musics from outside the West), his curating, and
in the work of the label. The idea of location in the context of
the world, of world music, undergoes a subtle shift, from being
about unity and harmony to revealing a much more interesting
and variegated set of practices that will in turn be opened up
to new combinatory potentials. In this way, even the simplest
statements of liberal hopefulness about connection, discovery,
respect and so on partake of a much more interesting ground that
is ever-mutating.

    This has a further repercussion for Gabriel as global inhabit-
ant – and it is about more than respecting difference in the context
of unity. Instead, the recognition of an essential, unavoidable
hybridity in music and culture tells us something about globalizing culture just as it was taking off in the late 1980s (in the form
of fast access to international cultural products, cheap travel,
the thawing of the Cold War and, maybe most importantly, the
move of high finance into the realm of electronic exchange) and
offers a theorization that parallels the spread of post-colonial
ideas. I would venture that, far from providing grist to that theoretical mill, Gabriel was an early adopter, even a precursor, of

post-colonial theorists' ideas about reconfiguring the West as just one part of a current de-hierarchized world system that can take stock of earlier, imperial globalizations.

Gabriel is of course no subaltern. This white, heterosexual, English male subject is not living in inherited oppression or discrimination. Maybe he has benefited from previous and/or persistent inequalities and violence, on a global scale. But far from being neo-imperialist in approach, Real World understands that it intervenes in a world riven by histories. It knows and reflects on the positionality of being a UK-based company with access to global markets, and Gabriel and his collaborators choose to collaborate with musicians from the world *without distinction*. Critics may think he has extracted value from the subjects garnered for Real World. If so, the logical position would be that it would be better for Westerners not to mingle so freely and to stay within some sort of non-intervention box, or perhaps to withhold the connection to a capitalist market. It is much better to avoid adopting generalist positions and instead to look at Gabriel's actual practice as it occurs in the context of a liberal utopianism, which is in turn defined through specific practices. The collaboration and use of various genres in *Passion* was explored earlier, and now I turn to *Passion: Sources*, the curious companion to that album.

For the soundtrack of *The Last Temptation of Christ*, Gabriel used new recordings, collaborations with a vast array of musicians, adaptations of traditional songs and sounds, and also field recordings from the present and sourced from library recordings. The material was re-edited for the release under his own name (*Passion*) and as *Passion: Sources*. The latter album contains no playing or composing by Gabriel, and gives space for the musicians that worked with him either to provide their own track of choice, or re-present the work that was included in the film. Alongside those selections, it recognizes the original tracks that also featured in the film that had already been released, and in one case a live recording made on the set of the film in Morocco, and supplemented later by percussion from Manu Katché and Hossam Ramzy. As was the case with *Passion*, the musicians and music come from a wide range of locations – Egypt, Ethiopia, Senegal, Morocco, Guinea, Armenia, Iran, Turkey, Pakistan and India. The release thus mirrors the colour tab that Real World used as a label identifier at the edge of its covers, signalling through its 'rainbow' design the linking but not homogenizing of music from around the world. The album is dominated by percussion, vocals and wind instruments – no electric or electronic instruments were used, and no amplification other than that supplied in the action of microphone recording, as far as I can tell. So as well as establishing a unifying mood from the diverse contributions, a further connecting factor between the two albums is the use of acoustic instrumentation.

Acoustic instrumentation has become a signifier of authenticity, of liveness, and the connectedness of musician and instrument that symbolizes the connection between musician and their culture (even if we can extend that culture to include the one of 'the world' or of 'humanity'). But this album was not an acoustic product – like any album, it is caught up in the recording process, and ultimately it is a digital CD that is the product of a studio, equipped with electronic, electrical and digital components to ensure high-quality recording (this very concept being already a 'technology' that operates mutually with others in the production of music in the 'industry'). At the very least, the apparatus of capture took the music beyond the realm of the supposedly organic, acoustic soundworld. Given that this album was part of the first set of releases on the Real World label, it was also a flagship for the mission of Gabriel and his collaborators (particularly fellow compiler David Bottrill). While putting forward this range of music, 'both traditional and modern from all around the world', the album also promotes the studio in its own right, acting

as a business calling card: 'Our studios have been designed for the
artist, to provide a place for great work around which we hope to
build the label.'[2] It is clear then that this was not an act of chari-
table paternalism, but the prescient grasping of a nascent world
economy for music, where people would listen to 'exotic' music if
presented in forms that mirrored, without exactly replicating, the
structures of the traditional music companies of the time.

The musicians on the album had an interesting status:
through Gabriel's curation of the album (and involvement in
editing and producing), they became material contributors to a
single-album global jukebox, their specificities ceding to Gabriel's
vision. However, it is not evident that much was being lost in
being part of a compilation where there might well be a unifying
aesthetic, as the album clearly spends time delineating in detail the
origins, genres and usual locations of the types of music we hear,
as well as fully crediting musicians, library recordings, researchers.
That still leaves us with the word 'sources', though. In using this
word, Gabriel aimed to recognize the influences on his own work,
to bring out the original pieces and make them available to the
putative world music listener. But he was also implying that these
are musics whose place is to be inspiration for some other work
– the bedrock on which others may build. That this was not his
intention does not remove the implications of the identification
of some music as primordial 'source' for something more developed. Beyond that problematic word, though, this album needs
to be heard as a compilation like any other, or something akin to
a soundtrack pieced together by Quentin Tarantino – who tries
to compile sonic narratives from pre-existing and highly varied
sources. It would be a mistake to fret too much about possible
paternalism if this idea is only selectively applied to non-European
musicians who are getting paid, receiving royalties, getting benefit
from working with Gabriel and further exposure from Real
World. The library recordings are more problematic in this

regard, their 'sources' long left behind as part of a document (we could perhaps say the same of the 'Wedding Song' on *Passion: The Sources*, recorded 'in the field' in Morocco).

The hybridizing of music from different traditions and impulses is not as dominant in individual tracks as on *Passion*, but the whole is hybrid, grown from cross-fertilization. The album as a unified piece, as marker in the strategy of both Gabriel and his company, is there to stand as exemplar of the hybridization Real World seeks to encourage. Over the years, the label continued to do this with great success, always on the lookout for fusions of new and traditional styles, or new constructs based on musicians from very different backgrounds. Again, this Real World looks to counter the prevailing homogenization of a certain media culture with an emboldened assumption of mixing, or *métissage*, as a more meaningful and less top-down variety of the global. Gabriel's commercial power, at this point, due to *So* and its singles, meant that he could cross between the two worlds of globalization, or perhaps two modes of 'worlding'. The fruit of that crossing is a hybrid cluster of products – the album *Us*, and also the multimedia CD-ROM *Xplora1* (including the documentary *All About Us*, and also available on CD-i). Staying within the terrain marked out by *So*, the follow-up album incorporated the various branchings and linkages Gabriel had been working on in and around the soundtrack for *The Last Temptation of Christ*.

Us, released in 1992, marks something of a consolidation of *So* in terms of its musical approach, but the tracks are longer, broader (more layered) and richer in instrumentation. *Us* arrives into a world where popular music had become more eclectic, with 'independent' music, house, grunge, industrial, gangsta rap having shifted the landscape. Closer to Gabriel's mission, perhaps, was part of the growing sense of something that would be called 'post-rock', exemplified by Talk Talk's *Spirit of Eden* (1988), David

Sylvian's *Gone to Earth* (1986) and *Secrets of the Beehive* (1987), and instrumental 'rock' groups like Tortoise. Post-rock aspired to combine electronics with rock instrumentation and develop music that was experimental but reasonably tuneful, aiming for effect through extended musical form and purposely moving away from the pop song format. In hindsight, Gabriel – as well as Kate Bush – was exemplary in sharing this aim. Gabriel's non-soundtrack work had of course been highly narrative, and in the case of *Us*, confessional in its lyrical emphasis, but the length and layers of the songs take them far from standard forms of the pop or rock song.

Us follows up not only on *So*, but also on *Passion* and Gabriel's public and media interaction with the world, through the multiple activities outlined above. The title demonstrates clearly the album's role as culmination of a personal, political and musical exploration, one that moves from 'the other' (in many guises) as exotic to 'the other' being a companion in shared community. In discussing *So*, I brought out the move to openness that Gabriel sought to convey musically and lyrically, and the expression of that openness through often playful visualization. That album marked a step beyond the portrayal of border situations expressed in the *Peter Gabriel* albums, but was still about psychological reflection. In *Us*, Gabriel was to perform inward analysis and outward relations more directly – the word 'I' features constantly, as does the interest in barely concealed references to sex, in 'Steam' and 'Kiss That Frog'. On those two singles, which are among the more straightforward tracks on the album, we can almost hear the exhortation to 'express your sexual feelings openly, Peter' from some therapy session, but the punning in these tracks makes them more of a parallel to the analytic session than a response to it – as coding is still in play, even if consciously manipulated to bring out desire as motivation. The tug of competing forces that we heard in 'That Voice Again' on *So* has now become a source of positively oriented behavioural modification, as we can hear in 'Love to Be

Loved', where Gabriel addresses his own motivation in relationships and in the more formal therapeutic session, as the lyrics talk
of wanting to be needed, to be liked, to be loved. For good and
ill, this is a mature album – the years in gestation firming up the
thoughts, building layer upon layer of music in the studio – with
massive attention to the way Gabriel's own voice is heard, close
to the ear and taking much more of the available sound than had
mostly been the case on previous albums. Where that technique
was used for a whispered threat on earlier albums, it is now the
mode for delivering positive change on an intimate basis.

The openness needs to be heard as more than just self-realization or heightening of self-awareness, such that other people can
be accommodated and no longer be secondary to the narrator's
interior priorities. Gabriel's personal world is a microcosm of the
world he had been growing into, and is now hybrid in its own
right, a world of mixing that is not about loss or uncertain transformation, but, he said, about joining, about getting over

> The sense that there is a dividing line between 'us' and 'them'.
> The further back you can push the dividing line, the less prob-
> lems the world is going to have. The more people you feel
> compassion, sympathy and understanding for the better.[3]

It goes without saying that the self-expression of *Us* is highly
formalist – the vocal delivery, the work done on that voice in
the studio, the carefully constructed and relatively long songs.
Even 'Love to Be Loved', an apparently simple, gentle tune just
expressing a childlike wish to be liked, is highly constructed – it
is a self-conscious statement about his drives, but also an almost
exaggerated response to (self-)interrogation. This presentation of
emotions and wishes is couched as a weird love song, eschewing
the actual or direct personal need, to reflect on what he feels
he needs. If this song has a spatial or locational position, it is in

the midst of a warped and recursive dream in the style of M. C. Escher.

The embedding of this seemingly simple but reflective lyrical interest in music that performs a complex hybridity can sometimes be neglected in the 'craftedness' of *Us*. The music is very heavily textured – an overused word, perhaps, in music reviews – but here I mean something very specific, that the music establishes atmospheres within which the vocals occur. Gabriel has said that he 'was trying with this record to take a different approach and make things duller', so flattening and thickening the sound.[4] These atmospheres require longer-form songs to work, and provide the grain to the lyrical content. The music is there not as backup, but as establishing ground, hence its seeming 'quite heavy for a lot of people in terms of content and also sound', as Gabriel mused.[5] This background is capable of fluctuating, but always maintains a certain thickness. At a very simple level, this stems from each track involving large numbers of contributors, and each input has the capacity to rise to the front and make the track change direction.[6] This is just as well, as the album does have its ponderous moments, and as Daryl Easlea and others have pointed out, many of the songs are significantly improved live, by reduction to those more fluctuant parts (as seen in the *Secret World* DVD or CD from the 1993 tour, discussed below).

The album opens with the powerful 'Come Talk to Me' – a plea for openness and an imagined prospect wherein the narrator's own absolution and/or justification would be heard. The invitation to an other to come out of themselves and move towards Gabriel's narrating I is a statement of the recognition of the depth of others' perceptions and reactions. The aim is to reduce distance, to begin a communicating partnership. This is established in formal terms through the duetting presence of Sinéad O'Connor, and extends musically in the contributions of over a dozen musicians, as well as choral singers, and

instrumentation ranging from the duduk, heard prominently on
Passion, through bagpipes, and on into an array of percussion.
Add to this Gabriel and others (including electronic music producer William Orbit) supplying programmed drones and rhythms,
and the album's sense of coalescing and bringing together multiple inputs into a unity is audibly clear (transaudient, perhaps).
This process of bringing together performs the same role as the
lyrics, and serves to render the overall theme of the album, insofar as there is one. The attention to the music, and the cultural
mixing Gabriel engages with, are the means of adding depth to
the lyrics, already modified and mobilized by Gabriel's vocal staging, and also troubling the idea that this is simply a confessional
album.[7]

Beyond personal connections, what Gabriel is opening up
about is globalization, hybridity, a world made harmonious by
clashing and unexpectedly combining diverse sounds and voices
(such as the African drummers, and the Russian folk singing
revival group led by Dmitri Pokrovsky). 'Come Talk to Me' uses
some spatial metaphors – most notably the reaching 'out through
the border fence', to enrich the pulling inward of the 'you' named
in the song – but the more interesting space is created in the
sound, with Gabriel's voice high 'up' in the mix, creating the aural
illusion of proximity. At the same time, the rich swells of the
slowly mounting and increasingly thick musical texture are like
the aspic or resin that maintains spatial immersiveness.

In the 'Blood of Eden', Gabriel takes a biblical turn, stopping
off at the Christian Book of Genesis, and although religion crops
up later and references to 'darkness' pepper the album, this track
refers only obliquely to the myth of Eden, home to the first two
humans, Adam and Eve. In the myth, the Christian God banishes
the two humans for their acquisition of knowledge in the form
of sexual activity. The 'Blood of Eden' is all about restoring a lost
unity: in the lyrics Gabriel says 'the union of the woman and the

man', and in commenting on the song in the video *All About Us* he talks of 'when man and woman were in one body' (echoing the hermaphroditic adventure of the Genesis song 'The Fountain of Salmacis' and the bodily merging in their epic 'Supper's Ready'). In relation to the Garden of Eden story, this means that unity is only possible on the back of loss. The 'blood' of the title removes the origin story from a location outside time and space (Adam and Eve age and die only as a consequence of being made to leave) and repositions the union within the womb – a cycle of birth and rebirth – replacing the virtuous ignorance imposed by the Christian God with the arcane knowledge of opposites combining, time working in cycles of reincarnation and the mystical power of intercourse. This is a fleshy exploration of the world of consciousness that will continue in the following track, 'Steam', but 'Blood of Eden' should more properly be seen as part of the arc from 'Come Talk to Me' to the closing 'Secret World', wherein physical reflection and mental exploration track a dual and bonded relation to one another.

The divergence from Christianity appears in the presence of the medieval test for witchcraft, as the 'you' of 'Blood of Eden' presents an object that could be either 'dagger or crucifix', and then, more puzzlingly, in the one verse that addresses spiritual loss completely apart from the building and recasting of the 'Eden' of heterosexual sex. In this verse, 'I can hear the thunder of a million unheard souls' looking for 'creature comfort' 'for the filling of their holes'. The last line could signal the sex of the rest of the song, but seems very different, and not at all about union, but gratification. More likely, it is about the shallowness of consumer society, while also referring to the spiritual vacuum created by the absence of the God that was supposed to be listening. If this is so, then the return to (a new) Eden is an escape from a world voided of meaningful contact through the strictures of those who first came up with religious control. In other words, the language and concept of God is what took humanity away from harmonious, non-repressed living. This may be overstating Gabriel's position, but it is clear that a highly physicalized mode of exploration, combined with self-awareness and listening to others, constitutes a sort of agnostic pan-liberalism – within which he can show how 'two people . . . and all of us, as in people' can connect, through a 'merging of boundaries', as Gabriel said in *All About Us*.

The religious references continue in 'Only Us' and 'Washing of the Water'. In the former, the reference to angels is primarily interesting in the context of a new Eden, where 'I hear you calling me home from the great escape' – and so the I of the song hears better and better, literally being (re-)united through the sound of voices and the promise of firm location they bring. There is another side to 'only us', in terms of globalization and 'us', and that is the unity of all in the form of 'us', a joint entity. This is entirely consistent with Gabriel's philosophy and his practice of it, but has a hidden dimension if we think of the borders of 'us'. I do not mean the border of a nation, people or culture, but the possibility of a border even if 'we' are all part of 'us'. As Julia Kristeva points out, when the Stoics invented the idea of a universal cosmopolitanism in the third and second centuries BCE, it carried the implication that someone could remove themselves from this order, implying that exclusion could happen.[8] Religions based on conversions would spread the malign idea that because everyone can have access to the truth, those who are outside are not part of 'us'. Gabriel's phrasing of 'only us' (and therefore nothing more) extends the safe proximity of a couple together to all people – there will only be us, and no outside, no 'them'. Gabriel's exoticism, where he looks at and loves the other as other, falls away as a practice of mixing. This, then, becomes not just a banner of unity but a rigorous practice of hybrid culture, leading post-colonial theory in the shape of formal, commercial, practical and argued practice.

In 'Washing of the Water', baptism looms large, and sex swims in the streams of its lyrics, never far from the surface, but the idea of a river that carries the I of the song sets up another form of merging, this time with natural, desacralized water. The river's flow is dangerous; letting go feels wrong, the narrator continues; and in the end the lyrics dream of a different river, one that can dispense dreams and sleep, removing pain – very much like the river of Lethe in the Greek mythological location of Hades, even if those waters achieve their effect through being consumed as opposed to bathing. In this song and others, it is nature, or Nature, that becomes a cradling force, one that is inside as well as other, capable of uniting those two realms. Peculiarly, perhaps, after the water, we hear that Gabriel's 'I' has been rummaging in filth, in the hidden depths, in 'Digging in the Dirt' – a rare occasion on *Us* when Gabriel seems vocally

Still from 'Digging in the Dirt' music video, directed by John Downer.

immersed, as opposed to going along with its musical flow or reflecting on it as it goes along – it is the only time there is an attack in the delivery. After the ambient musings of 'Fourteen Black Paintings', which features a sparse Gabriel reflection on Mark Rothko's paintings in the Rothko Chapel, Houston, it is back (via the sideshow of 'Kiss That Frog') to the conclusion of the main arc of a kind of emotional ecology where Gabriel's personal openness and global involvement combine with a burgeoning sense of nature as another actor or agent in the world. 'Fourteen Black Paintings' represents a formal statement of that multiple-sourced conception – the chapel is open to all faiths, a kind of secularized religiosity under the aegis of Rothko's attempt at a universal reflection on life and death. The music ranges widely in its instrumentation, acting as a foil for the people that feature as the protagonist in the short song, ending with the line 'from the people come the power'. As well as tying in to Gabriel's political commitment to liberal (and anti-neoliberal) world politics, the power aimed for here is one of self-knowledge. That awareness is an aspiration not to be the centre of the universe, but the place where the universe can be seen and partially understood, as the subject achieves a kind of broader, almost non-subjective perspective. So, we might see the song as a conceptual antechamber to 'Secret World', and, like in 'Solsbury Hill', a very specific place stands in for a wider (or deeper) concern.

'Secret World' begins with exposure – 'I stood in this unsheltered place' – with the voice very present in the mix, and largely, carefully free, like natural make-up, of effects. This exposure has brought the narrator to some sort of enlighten-ment – one that brings a return to a reconfigured Eden, where the scission between Adam and Eve is fixed, sexual union taken away from the *nomos* or jurisdiction of religion and brought to a new location, where 'the house is crumbling but the stairways stand' – paths and journeys persist as the controlling structure fades. That particular line occurs in the exuberant bridge, the lyrics of which begin with a wheel turning endlessly, recounted over a rippling bass line and thick keyboard chords, along with the ever-present and bass-oriented percussion, which supplies a continually changing presence through the song. The status of the location changes, but in another return, we also hear the recuperation of marginal spaces that featured so prevalently in *Peter Gabriel*, 1980 iteration. Here, 'railways sidings' feature, as a place for illicit embrace, as part of the reconquest of a harmonious and consensually sullied garden, fertilized by a positive and liberal perspective on how individuals, cultures and ecology might interact, if given the chance to build reflectively. 'Secret World' restores the big beats of the opening 'Come Talk to Me' and pushes on from the warmly soporific shuffle in the defamiliarized garden of 'Blood of Eden'.

By this stage of his career, Gabriel was no longer entertaining the idea of an album as a standalone release. The album itself featured commissioned artworks for each song, provided by different artists, which appeared as part of the album's artwork. There were also artist-made videos for some of the tracks. True to Gabriel being ahead of the liberal variant of globalization, these artists were not chosen only from the Western art world and practices. This decision to curate Western and non-Western artists together is something that the art world still imagines to be a bold new move, a quarter of a century later. *Us* saw parallel releases of *All About Us*, on LaserDisc and vhs cassette, and the cd-rom *Xplora1*, whose expanded version also contained *All About Us*. In 1992–3, the idea of expanded releases was in its infancy – we were not beset by the endless bloating of classic albums (a process that began in the early twenty-first century, picking up steam after 2010), nor was it the norm to fill 78 minutes of a cd, let alone produce innovative visual components. There were, of course, intricate music videos for *Us*, much along the lines of those of *So*, and a highly advanced stage collaboration with the Canadian theatre and multimedia director Robert Lepage for the 'Secret World' tour, which brought Gabriel's development of a show to its most complex since *The Lamb Lies Down on Broadway*. Intervening tours had been lightly conceptualized and, as we saw in the 'This Way Up' tour, were increasingly about putting on a big spectacle that bent the rules of rock performance, undermining stadium rock through humorous deflation of stock moves and expectations. 'Secret World' began to work in a new dimension for a rock album, enabled by new technologies and a sense that music should not be left to just be itself in a live setting, because this too would be a staging, one that would merely replicate the machinery put in place for major tours. Instead, the preparation would go not into what Alan White of Yes has called 'high performance' music, but into self-conscious multimedia staging, after what Gabriel described as a decision to 'spend some years in a visual wilderness to get the musical foundation sorted out'.[9]

The concerts featured video and technological elements, but it is the staging that drove the show. Videos play behind the songs, often indicating in quite literal fashion the title or theme of them, and the layout of the stage allows considerable physical interpretation of the songs. The stage is divided into a round part and a square part, connected by a long walkway, which also contains a rolling travelator. The two stages represent masculine and feminine, and also transformation, as Lepage, according to Gabriel, thought that 'most of what I was writing about was transformation.'[10] The different performance areas are used to emphasize developments and changes within the music or lyrics. The movement of Gabriel and band is used to heighten not just the plotlines of songs but to echo the psychological locatedness of Gabriel and his narrators, in relation to, or separation from, others (with the group dancing of 'Shaking the Tree' and 'In Your Eyes' thereby becoming much more powerful statements of togetherness, social unity and of an *Us*. This happens from the beginning, with the extensive use of a phone box in the opening track 'Come Talk to Me'. Gabriel sings the verses from inside the brightly lit, traditional red British phone box, in an accidentally ironic take on the development of new technologies – with UK telecoms subject to privatization at the time, as an exemplar of Thatcherism's drive to bring everything on to the market, the red box symbolized steady, familiar and reliable communication. As he emerges, he pulls on the semi-rigid cable and stretches out towards backing singer Paula Cole on the other stage. Through the song, he pulls closer and then is dragged back along the travelator. The staging actually delimits the meaning of the lyric to the one simple idea of Gabriel trying to talk to someone in order to get her to reply. The drawing back to the box does provide an interesting supplement, in that it shows that the attempt to communicate needs channelling, whether verbal, therapeutic or technological.

'Digging in the Dirt' extends the use of close-up camera that first appeared in the 'This Way Up' tour. Gabriel uses a head-mounted camera to provide extreme close-ups of his face, particularly the eyes, and also his head movements. These are then projected to be seen at much increased scale. The distortions and the close-up itself are both significant, conceived as means of emphasizing the strangeness of self-reflection, the changes in perspective it can bring. More interestingly, the projection defies the convention that the screens at a stadium rock gig are there to provide visual information that your place in the mass withholds, and Gabriel was consciously inspired by U2's use of screens, but also sought to do something different:

I was originally planning an all-out video assault, with flying
screens and stuff, but then I saw the U2 *Zoo tv* tour in America
– I saw it five times actually – and the visual intelligence there
was so strong I thought maybe I shouldn't be trying a video
spectacular.[11]

With the integration of stage performance and close camerawork
of 'Digging in the Dirt', the comforting illusion of watching from
a distance is broken, replaced by a glimpse into the more chaotic
process of the dirt-digging of self-investigation.

'Secret World' uses the screen that hovers above the stage to
full effect, with a shimmering Gabriel announcing the existence
of mysterious places as it turns over, in reflection of 'the wheel
is turning, spinning round and round', along with a strobing
effect for the more powerful refrain sections. Gabriel leads the
band into suitcases, and they descend secretly on a small ele-
vator under the stage. The secret world is revealed to be a true
destination, but not the resolution of an arduous quest. The
whole trick recalls film pioneer Georges Meliès' film *Le Locataire
diabolique* (The Diabolic Tenant, 1909), a colour film in which
the tenant of the title brings out a host of objects and his family
from a large suitcase, to which they all will be returned as the
film progresses. Méliès was significant in film history in that he
was very much a liminal figure, navigating between different
genres of magic, music hall, live performance, theatre and film.
Close to a hundred years later, this trick could only be seen as
a means of expressing the idea that Gabriel is just such a figure
too. As the song closes on Gabriel, a domed tent descends, to
be followed by the re-emergence of the group for 'Don't Give
Up'. The transition to that point via the dome suggests that the
prospect for a secret world lies in a future that arrives through
protection, and final re-emergence.

Finally, in the world of *Us* comes the CD-ROM (also CD-i)

Xplora1, a time capsule of a tech future and also of tech futurism. Gabriel, enthusing about his multimedia projects at the time, said,

> there's a whole culture around future technology, the trippy end of which I call the cyber world – virtual reality, CD-ROM and all that – which reminds me of the '60s sense you'd get from *Oz* and *IT* [*International Times*] of wide open frontiers.[12]

To encounter this piece is to engage with a world akin to that found in William Gibson's *The Peripheral*, where a sort of time travel happens through a retooling of games and parallel timestream virtual reality technology.[13] To explore the CD-ROM today entails sending the already defunct iMac into its earliest, 'classic' mode. Once there, a host of activities and glimpses into Gabriel's multiple interests appear.

To access the full content first requires piecing together Gabriel's face from parallel fragments; to go further involves selecting these fragments in newly dispersed form, clearly referencing his history of facial misrecognition (the covers of the *Peter Gabriels*, the video for 'Sledgehammer', the masks and make-up on various tours). Beyond that, the player can also find out about Amnesty and the then recently launched Witness project (giving the means of recording to individuals so that they could film and document abuses of power), as well as WOMAD and Real World. *Xplora1* explicitly extends the reach of *Us*, while connecting to imagery used on the 'Secret World' tour. At the same time it takes the releases of the label into the informatic dimension.

Like *Us*, the CD-ROM travels inwards psychologically and in coded game space, while opening up internal, fractal dimensions. That certainly sounds hyperbolic, but if we reflect back to 1993,

Box for Gabriel's multimedia disc project *Xplora1*.

effectively before the Internet, let alone media embedding, it feels
very much ahead of its time. Games were heading in this direction, but the idea of hyperlinking separate parts of information,
music, video and game features was highly innovative. *Xplora1*
does more than show the opening up of unexpected inner dimensions; it also mirrors the processes of technological change that
accompany burgeoning capitalistic globalization. In the future, as
seen from there, all would be connected, accessible, multimedia
and loaded with extras. On a discursive level, the interactivity of
Xplora1, which is certainly very clunky, is also oddly familiar in that
we have seen all the formatting, content and navigation on this
disc become habitual. It is too easy to assume that IT communications would inevitably have moved forward via Web 2.0 towards
social media. The outlier contribution that is *Xplora1* illustrates on
the contrary that the belief in the value of interactivity precedes
the technology that would later 'allow' it. Gabriel is of course an
optimist, and the processes of 'sharing' are an exemplary statement, at a micropolitical level, of wider changes and directions for
individual and social interaction.

Within the *Us* section, videos for the singles 'Digging in the
Dirt', 'The Blood of Eden', 'Kiss that Frog' and 'Steam' appear.
The videos make extensive use of digital filming and editing
techniques, and just as the viewer might wonder if parallel
Gabriels are forever stuck in eternal returns of stop-motion,
another picture emerges, which is that the highly saturated
videos, in being gathered here, suggest further 'secret worlds',
while in the 'real world' of their more familiar MTV presence
they are seen as interpreting and perhaps heightening the song's
lyrics, mood or theme. These embedded future worlds are like
recursive time capsules within the larger one of *Xplora1* – worlds
within worlds – again illustrating the individual connecting to
the global. Inside this global fractal machine, the depiction of
Witness makes more sense as something highly contemporary.
Launched by Gabriel on 23 March 1992, the idea of Witness
was and is to encourage the recording of violence, oppression
and illegal or illegitimate behaviour where reporting is strictly
controlled or discouraged by menace, and it does this through
sharing the machinery and the means of dissemination.[14] The
organization has become huge in the intervening quarter-
century, and surely it does not need saying that tucked away in
this CD-ROM is an explosive indicator of a future – unlike that of
the outmoded hybrid format of *Xplora1* – that has come to pass.
Ironically or not, the success of Witness has been outstripped by
the forces of capitalist production of ever newer portable technology, and increasing levels of monetized communication, such
that hand-held phones or very basic computers are linked to the
means of communication. It is a simple fact that Gabriel has
often been at the cutting edge of technology, and, in different
ways, of globalization. What is of interest is how this engagement matches and drives on the thinking that underlies both
his music and his possibly over-optimistic liberal universalism.

On all fronts in the early 1990s, Gabriel was getting closer to the world and somehow travelling inward at the same time, opening up the prospect of deeper communications at personal and global levels, as they intertwined.

7 THE LOCAL IN THE GLOBAL, THE GLOBAL IN THE LOCAL

In the series of deterritorializations, defamiliarizations and delocalizations of Gabriel's career tracked thus far, I have tried to move on from some of the suspicions critics might have about a commercially successful Western musician working with musicians from outside the rock and pop of that sector of the world. I have tried to bring out the deep connections between the range of Gabriel's activities and the lyrical, formal and media concerns to be heard and seen in his recordings and performances. There is a recognition that while his activity can be criticized as being beholden to Enlightenment values, in his case, almost no writers are willing to directly declare him a stooge of imperialist capitalism. Others have been willing to impute a hierarchy where 'musicians of the rest of the world' are in some way subaltern, and are silenced (as Gayatri Spivak tells us of the colonial situation) in the wake of Gabriel using his name as the artist for his albums.

In tune with Gabriel's work in assembling groups of his own that featured musicians from numerous locations, post-colonial thought has long advocated the idea of hybridity, of collapsing identities as a way of critiquing old colonially imposed situations. The process of identifying, particularly when done from the outside, in the name of the universal, values of tolerance, freedom, equality and so on, has also come in for close critical scrutiny, on the grounds that these values have often acted to legitimize the processes of global imperialism. For Homi Bhabha, writing of hybridity as a way of avoiding the traps of fixed, unchanging and unitary identity, 'these "inbetween" spaces provide the terrain for elaborating strategies of selfhood – singular or communal – that initiate new signs of identity.'[1] The then current moment (of the early 1990s) presented 'overwhelming evidence of a more transnational and translational sense of the hybridity of imagined communities'.[2] These ideas go against ideas of 'authenticity' and raise the possibility of thinking about music as always already hybrid, not spontaneously and uniquely generated, and that encounters between cultures did not have to involve exploitation or ruin. Gabriel was and remains an absolute advocate for such 'mixing', and we can refer back to Steven Feld's idea of 'schizophonia' as something much more positive. It is through this lens that I will consider the mass collaborations that are *Big Blue Ball* (2008, mostly recorded 1991, 1992 and 1995) and *ovo* (2000), closing on Gabriel's own *Up* (2002) as an album that occurs in a critically hybrid space he has cleared.

Hybridity represents a recognition of difference that does not say, 'you are different', but instead that we share a set of differences that locate us and provide creative forces for inter-action. Hybridity is a complex issue for 'world music', whether as marketing term or as more honestly felt global utopianism, because if 'we' (any 'we') are looking to hear the other, the exotic, the new, then its difference, or its specificity, could be important. Artists everywhere, however, often love using forms *they* have taken from elsewhere, short-circuiting the keen globalist liberal's sense of being the great discoverer of previously hidden sounds. In 2014, reflecting on 25 years of Real World as a label, and musing on new hybrid forms, Gabriel said that 'within every country there are good hip hop artists who quite often integrate some of the local music' – but also that the rest of Real World's management were resistant to the label going down that path.[3] Both locally and internationally, questions of authenticity riddle any music that wishes to be traditional, 'roots', or true to some sort of heritage, with or without reference to world music. Furthermore, until prompted, many musicians often claim to pay no heed to the geographical locatedness of their music, and Real World has maintained a policy of encouraging hybrid, mixed musics even before setting up collaborative recordings.

Real World was, and still is, interested in what it imagines to be real 'roots' music, but was never shy of propagating its own mixes of musicians as well as styles, as in the fusion group Afro Celt Sound System, or one of the label's most successful albums, *Night Song* (1996) by Nusrat Fateh Ali Khan and Michael Brook, also featuring musicians from beyond the two named performers' home continents of Asia and North America. Explicitly hybrid or no, world music is not free from curation, a selection process that is not decided by the 'world' musician but by editors, musicians, record label bosses, producers.[4] Eclectic expertise from the point of view of the universal global is never far away. Simon Frith further argues that the idea of world music drove a belief in the *value* of hybridity, such that cultural mixing 'defines hybridity as authenticity and implies that musical creativity depends on a free trade in sounds'.[5] Pop music of the 1990s, perhaps not always in awareness of Bhabha and other philosophers of hybridity / multiplicity, or even Gabriel, saw a massive upsurge in transcultural music, heavily driven by the possibilities of digital sampling, re-editing and mixing.[6] Much of this was tokenistic, opportunistic or ill-conceived, just like any other musical production. I am not about to exclude Gabriel from having been part of a period's fashion for the cosmopolitan. What I am not going to say is that his particular open sense of location can be construed as politically suspect because of its openness. But Frith's point about the 'free trade of sounds' resonates strongly today – a liberal belief in the

freeness of music cannot entirely escape the tethers of neoliberal
markets.

Musicologists Georgina Born and David Hesmondhalgh
have little time for the valorization of hybridity, taking it as an
expression of bad faith, based on theoretical models they find
uncomfortable. They wrote (in 2000) that 'the current trend is
toward the celebration of hybridities without end.'[7] This is not
praise, as the word 'celebration' has long been a code word for the
removal of credibility from the thing being celebrated, from the
celebrator, and from the practice of celebrating that the irrespon-
sible and unserious were engaged in. Much less superficial is their
fuller statement about the embrace of hybridity:

> The implication is that these hybrid aesthetics and movements
> are free of the earlier hierarchical consciousness and practice,
> that there are no significant 'core-periphery' structures at
> work, and thus that these aesthetics are free also of the asym-
> metrical relations of representation and the seductions of
> the exoticism, primitivisms, and Orientalisms that paralleled
> colonial and neocolonial relations.[8]

There is plenty here that could be whittled down to simple
presumption, but the overall position is compelling: there is
no way out, ultimately, for anyone. But this does not make all
non-Westerners who make music into victims, voiceless, exploited
or incapable of making misrepresentation. These 'structures'
can be criticized in all cultural activity, no matter how much it
is hedged. But it would seem that even if Gabriel cannot escape
power relations (nobody can), he can work with them consciously
in non-exploitative, even-handedly collaborative ways.

Another concern that I think is dealt with by Gabriel's work
leading up to 2000 is that of 'schizophonia'. Feld's take on this
term has been vital and influential for reflection on world music,

or on appropriations of music from other areas of the world to one's own, particularly if operating from the wealthier part and 'borrowing' from a culture you can effectively use as a marketable commodity without recompense. As should be clear by now, Gabriel is not so much appropriating as working with elements from non-Western cultures, happy to create fusion-based styles that actually reward the skills of musicians from whichever part of the world they were born in. In this sense, the non-Western styles or musics that Gabriel in some way co-opts should not be taken differently to any other employment of musicians or to any influence from Western pop genres. To assume it would be different is to impose a 'subaltern' status on those the critic would seek to protect.

Gabriel's outlook on non-Western music, particularly from Africa, which most influences him, moved from a purposeful and respectful exoticism to a point where those 'other' musics were simply part of his world – by 1999, he was identifying world music as 'simply music that is played in the world'.[9] By the 1990s, Gabriel was no longer looking inward, or reaching outward; instead there was a greater sense of containment and connection, on the basis of a more simple, less clashingly hybrid sense of the direction of his own identity than before. Hybridity was established as already present; it has always already arrived and settled in, establishing a new fusional base. The sense of dis-location reduces, in other words – and that is why I return to the idea of 'schizophonia', which I have argued earlier should be seen as containing positive potential, if consciously and freely mobilized by artists, but less so if hastily adjudged to be essentially problematic. In a slightly fuller approach to the idea than he proposes elsewhere, Feld identifies the problem as being with what happens to the schizophonic sound, not the sound itself:

> By 'schizophonic mimesis' I want to question how sonic copies, echoes, resonances, traces, memories, resemblances,

imitations, and duplications all proliferate histories and possibilities. This is to ask how sound recordings, split from their
source through the chain of audio production circulation
and consumption, stimulate and license renegotiations of
identity.[10]

In particular, Feld has in mind the use of sampling and the tortuous ways 'field recordings' or tunes from 'elsewhere' crop up
as unquestioned and largely unpaid source material in Western
music, across a range of genres (many of which are outside
straightforward 'proper' rock). It is not the borrowing, the use as
inspiration, the adoption of techniques as such that bother Feld
in this essay, rather it is the more pragmatic question of ownership, of exploitation, as clearly demonstrated through under- or
non-payment and the blatant use of 'structural hierarchy'
between an industry based in the West and a less formal economy
elsewhere (in financial terms) of music production. Gabriel's
crediting of and collaboration with music and musicians arguably
could be seen as simply removing him from this problem. Gabriel
has negotiated these issues in ways that are consistently in tune
and time with, even ahead of, much post-colonial critique within
music.

   In 1991, 1992 and 1995, Real World organized three 'recording
weeks', which brought together a huge number of musicians – 75
in the first week, for example – and with well over fifty musicians
on *Big Blue Ball*, this album tries to replicate the collaborative and
exploratory feel of those events while also seeking to apply a
consistent aesthetic. Even with its belated release in 2008, it represented something of a flagship of the era in which Real World
became successful, and was a much more satisfying expression of
its mission than many of the more standard compilations the label
has brought out. With *Big Blue Ball*, Real World went from being
a collector to being a curator of live interaction between different

musics. Forcefully pushing an agenda of social hybridization, Real World signals the range of participants:

> Among the united nations of performers who found their way to Real World during those weeks were Billy Cobham, Papa Wemba, Hossam Ramzy and the Egyptian String Ensemble, Sinéad O'Connor, Natacha Atlas, flamenco guitarist Juan Canizares, American singer Joseph Arthur, Afro Celts James McNally and Iarla Ó Lionárd, Japanese percussionist Joji Hirota, Jah Wobble, gospel group The Holmes Brothers, Justin Adams, Francis Bebey, Tim Finn, Marta Sebestyen, guitarist Vernon Reid, Chinese flute player Guo Yue.[11]

Peter Gabriel's presence was a given, as was that of co-deviser of the project Karl Wallinger. The more well-known musicians were privileged by simply being named, and in the case of others, a further cultural and/or stylistic marker was added. The 'united nations' implied not only diversity but egalitarian collaboration. Power relations were not removed – this assembly is made possible in the domain of Peter Gabriel and his Real World studios. Production duties were shared by him and Wallinger. Yet again, though, those power relations were used reflectively as enabling tools. As the philosopher-historian Michel Foucault noted of power, it is productive – of every social situation, not just one of rigid hierarchy.

Dis-location had long represented a core feature of Gabriel's music by the time of the recording weeks at Real World. But almost in recognition that dislocation could induce a more problematic mode of schizophonia for musicians in different contexts outside the dominant music industry, *Big Blue Ball* represented a re-location in literal, spatial terms that necessitates a new term, perhaps *allophonia*, where different sounds work together in tandem and relocate in paired relation to each other.

One of the curious effects of this allophonia is not the flattening of difference but the flattening effect of hearing difference as normal, expected, reliable. In practical terms, the album displays a vast range of musical styles, albeit all working from initial templates of eight-minute grooves, according to Wallinger.[12] The production, with its emphasis on low-end dynamics and establishing rhythms first, does bring a unity to the album, but this is not the flattening factor. The perceived homogenizing (or homophonia) lies in the complete absence of surprise generated when the album moves from a track that combines African and European sounds to one that is basically rock, with other tracks featuring elements from across the continents, including from musicians already involved in using 'global' sounds, such as the French electronic band Deep Forest, who were massively successful 'fusion' artists in their own right in the 1990s. The fact that by the time of the album's release in 2008 we should have been so familiar with this prospect is an ironic success attributable in no small part to Gabriel and Real World. It also told us about music of the whole world, as opposed to either globalized (i.e. chart) music or world music – and that is that the listener can hear what Kofi Agawu refers to as the 'strategic embrace of sameness' that allows cross-fertilization or hybridizing in the first place.[13] What Agawu means is not just that all music is somehow the same, but that in order to hear or make music across cultures, there must be a presumption of shared language.[14] In the case of *Big Blue Ball*, the shared language is one that understands improvising practice to lead to a recognizable communal structure (the completed song, and then album).

Gabriel's presence is primarily one of host, appearing on five tracks (of eleven), and singing on only three. The album carries no artist name, nor does it propose that it is by 'various artists', so the commercial gain of Gabriel's presence is offset by that absence. Nonetheless, the opening song, 'The Whole

Thing', does talk about the world, and does connect to the cover concept. It also reveals the extensive and democratic accrediting of track composition, in being written by Alexis Faku, Tim Finn, Peter Gabriel, Geoffrey Oryema, Karl Wallinger and Andy White (though not Francis Bebey, whose contribution to the track is singled out on the album cover proper, and features 'pygmy flute'). The track echoes some of the subtly deconstructive lyrics that feature on *So* and *Us*.[15] Ostensibly a song about love, comparing love and dreams, while sung in a clear, reflective tone, it is also about self-reliance, as the world can continue in your absence. This can either be taken as offering a sense of wonder at the scale of the world, or of a self-awareness of the limits of solitary existence. But the fact that the world is simply 'out there', beyond the 'you' or 'I', does not mean it is separated off – far from it, as the world (and 'you') are in the dreams that infiltrate the narrator's mind. Self-awareness of the mutual separatedness of humans means that re-unifying, becoming a community through difference, is possible.

The cover of *Big Blue Ball* shows us a presumably digitally produced image of a big blue ball in a field of cows – the world comes to Albion, and Albion recognizes it has always been part of that ball that sits recursively in an enclosed field. The world comes to southwestern Britain, and so world music receives a (temporary) location at the Box studios, while remaining whole. The 'big blue ball' of the title suggests Carl Sagan's 'pale blue dot' – the image taken by the Voyager probe (on 14 February 1990), on his prompting, of Earth seen as a one-pixel-size blue dot, as a means of showing us the perspective that human scientific thinking had made possible.[16] Like Gabriel, Sagan was a liberal utopian and saw technology as something that only made sense if the rest of humanity could benefit. While this view has its limits, what we see in this big blue ball is the possibility not of encompassing the world, but making the world the object of our *activity*. This filters

Cover of the collaborative album *Big Blue Ball*, built from sessions with musicians using the Real World studios.

down into the practice of this collaborative project and album, where the whole is massive, a mass production, but each part is the effort of a different though not separate group. Each track is by a new combination of musicians, and they interlock, as groups recombine, relocating within the project. So at a pragmatic level, a social model for communal, provisional music-making is established in *Big Blue Ball*, one that uses 'schizophonia' in order to mutate it, to make it a willed activity by all, rather than just by the archiving audio anthropologist.

Where *Big Blue Ball* set the world in the field, amid nature (even if showing us a human-constructed environment of demarcated fields and the presence of purpose-bred animals), *ovo* was about making the world present in an urban version of globalized locatedness. Gabriel's project for London's Millennium Dome tracked a mythical history that was supposed to stand in for the story of industrialization, and was part of the celebrations of the arrival of the year 2000 CE. This project represented another collaborative venture where the album featured a vast number of musicians, and the event itself engaged a further large group of performers, including people working on the visual and structural part of the spectacle. *ovo* was vertical, historical, where *Big Blue Ball* is horizontal, geographical. The former tracked a story of questionable progress through time, the album matching this narrative drive, ending in an overcoming of the idea of false progress, while the latter album sought to cut a contemporaneous slice through global musical culture of the 1990s. *ovo* reflected less on its own structures of making – Gabriel's name was back, Gabriel wrote all the tracks, and the musicians performed as his group members, even if group membership shifted from track to track and often extended beyond the core of Tony Levin, Manu Katché and David Rhodes.

I will return later to the specific locatedness of the spectacle that Gabriel devised with Simon Fisher and 'assistance' from his established collaborator Robert Lepage. Suffice to say that the show tried to encompass movement, material stagecraft and digitally produced visuals as well as Gabriel's music. The show tried to mesh traditional and contemporary elements that would, said Gabriel, 'draw on the cultural origins of the many peoples who now comprise contemporary British culture', combining costumes, dances, styles of music.[17] In trying to occupy the dome space, a lot of literally high-level performance and visuals sought to direct the eye away from the two-plane restriction of much that is traditionally stage-based. Arguably, the presence of 'sky people' and of machines like 'the nest that sailed the sky' in the narrative of *ovo* was a product of the spatial nature of the host building.

The story takes place in three parts, representing a 'Big History' view of civilization, where culture moves from

agriculture and connectedness to nature, through an industrial
society that is productive, creative, but ultimately alienating, on
to a utopian prospect of life beyond the confines of apparent
progress, where a new, technologically driven harmony with the
ecosphere (or ecodome, like that of the Eden Project) is revealed
as future potential. This reductionism on a massive scale ties in to
many eschatological systems of thinking, but is notable for clearly
not ascribing any validity or tangible meaning to the bureau-
cratized service capitalism that contemporary Britain and the
London Dome would represent for many critics, in the absence of
having any mission or long-term purpose.[18] This grand tale is then
focused through the prism of one family, safely characterized by
long-standing gender-attributed roles: the father works stubbornly
with nature; the mother weaves and scries the future; the son
wants to break free through industry, while the daughter falls in
love. Only ovo, child of illicit love and whose name Gabriel said
comes from the human face (O for eyes, V for nose and ridge
atop nose) as opposed to an egg, eludes these restraints as he sails
off into the sky of the future (possibly one where the dome has
crumbled to allow escape). The guiding story was told by Neneh
Cherry and Rasco, with Gabriel interjecting, in 'The Story of
ovo' (track 1 on the ordinary CD release; bonus dual disc on the
special edition), and supplied a lot more detail than would have
been visible in the physical/material performance itself, or indeed
in the lyrics of the album.

ovo was something of a bridge between Gabriel's soundtracks
and his 'song' albums. There are several long instrumental sections, featuring numerous musicians from around the world, and
an extensive and dynamic use of percussion. Four main singers
(Paul Buchanan, Elizabeth Fraser, Alison Goldfrapp and Richie
Havens) share the vocals with Gabriel, playing the central characters, though Iarla Ó Lionáird also supplies vocals and presumably
the lyrics in Irish (uncredited on the CD). Traditional elements rub

shoulders with digital percussion, drones, editing and even early EDM (electronic dance music). Drums, brass and strings give the whole a very full-spectrum sound, and this means that even more musicians were involved than on *Big Blue Ball*. As noted above, the music and lyrics were very much under the control of Gabriel. The abstraction of those lyrics means that while they might aspire to general relevance, they do not get much of a foothold in significance. It is only occasionally that the listener gets a sense of the development of Gabriel's conceptions of place in the words themselves, even if plenty is going on around them in terms of the precise location of the event. Early on, 'The Time of the Turning' identifies the passing of seasons, with the first iteration of the song presenting the acceptance of the cyclical inevitability of seasons, the second more about the passing of things, with Goldfrapp singing that you can 'feel it all slipping away'. Gabriel's more personal 'Father, Son' closes the section on the era of agriculture, reflecting on the reassurance of family connection – a long way from the more intense and barbed thoughts on personal connection elsewhere in his career, and sounding here a bit like a paean to patrilineal power.

Given the physical locatedness of the show, in an epic, unloved and expensive government project, it is interesting that a monumental building features heavily in the middle part of the show and album – with 'The Tower that Ate People' expressing the danger of mechanized society, destroying its peons even as it reaches to the sky ('we're building up and up' is stated four times by Gabriel, in clear voice, where the bulk of the song is in his voice but heavily processed). This building echoes the supposed hubris in the tower that would become known as the Tower of Babel, where the Christian God struck down the building work and in so doing also created linguistic diversity. Ultimately, in *ovo*, a new, less uniform society emerges that had forged itself out of the destruction of the tower. If this is the

phallus tumbling, perhaps it is also the rejection of the patri-
archal rule established earlier. In 'White Ashes', the 'building
comes crumbling down', again sung by Gabriel in treated-voice
mode. At this point, it is hard not to imagine some presence
of critique for the Dome project itself, an opening salvo in the
'improvement' of southeast London, with further 'progress'
ahead (and now behind us) in the form of the Olympic stadium
and its legacies of debt, non-utility and even less participation in
sport than before.

Following the collapse of 'the building', the nest that carries ovo opens the prospect of a new world, echoing that of
'The Secret World'. The closing track, 'Make Tomorrow', sees
Buchanan, Fraser and Havens take vocal turns before Gabriel sings
the section that is about extreme dislocation, moving beyond the
planet. This dislocation is that of perspective, as he muses, 'you
wonder what they're all struggling for', before leading into a reit-
eration of 'make tomorrow today' as a call to utopian pragmatics
(and as seen in Gabriel's political engagements in Amnesty or
Witness). The song sails off into an extended instrumental, and
the spectacle concludes.

ovo spoke long of London and its Dome, at the Millennium
of 2000 CE. It tried to bring out the current nature of contemporary Britain as something that was not insular, not resistant to
change, and whose folk musics now looked outward, or indeed
inward, to a new location in Britain. The city is what Saskia Sassen
has identified as a global city, a set of vectors and processes that
have a lot to do with capitalism, but also with more cultural
forms of mobility and with the connectedness of technology.[19]
London in this reading becomes a node within a global system of
intertwining connections. Within the big story of ovo, this reading
of the future of culture struggles somewhat to get out, but it is
there. Its presence undermines the low-grade post-purpose mon-
umentalism of the Dome in favour of an unstitching of place as

The Millennium Dome Show, London, 2000, for which Gabriel composed the soundtrack, released as *ovo*.

something fixed. With *ovo*, the global city supplements the world in the village (think ship in a bottle) of *Big Blue Ball*.

Beyond those two projects lay the more traditional one of a 'standard' Peter Gabriel album, *Up*, which came out in 2002, after many years in the making, in parallel to the work on *ovo*. Scale was still a vital part of the album and accompanying 'Growing Up' tour, but moved from the world-striding multimedia epic of the millennial to a more focused rendering of contemporary concerns. The album and show divided, with the former focusing, at first hearing, on death, and prospects for life beyond the mundane, then revealing darker yet more interesting themes. The show was more complex and varied, with different ideas and machinery for many of the songs, extending the reach of the stadium concert into a highly technologized zone of activity. The prominent use of several pre-programmed tracks, layers and sounds heightened the immersion into technology. A key part of the performance was the central, round stage with encircling travelator feature. Above the stage, a host of objects awaited their descent, as well as the projection of images onto their surfaces. These included a second stage, with guardrail, an egg-shaped balloon and numerous screens. Gabriel would walk upside down on the upper stage ('Downside Up'), bounce in a giant hamster ball (the zorb ball), ride a bicycle, and go over, under, sideways round in a strangely serene technological fairground. The two stages symbolized heaven and earth, said Gabriel in 'The Story of Growing Up' on the *Growing Up Live* DVD, and also made the show (literally) revolve around vertical movements, transitioning from this world to another.

Away from the localized worlds summoned in *Big Blue Ball* and *ovo*, the tour nonetheless sought to capture the world's enmeshedness in technology – the continual reference to enclosure, even if assumed voluntarily, illustrated our containment in webs of technological power much better than the banal complaints about reality TV of 'The Barry Williams Show' from *Up*. The visual and digital technologies extended beyond the stage into the making of the DVD, which is described as being a 'film by Hamish Hamilton and Peter Gabriel', often using a horizontally split screen to show a sort of parallel engineering world. Effects and images from the physical concert sprawl out of the concert and onto the screen, in an over-directed, somewhat counterproductive excess. Around the group rush orange-clad engineers and camera crew, emerging and descending through trapdoors to move props, to film, or to wrangle cable. It is hard not to see

the orange outfits in the context of the post-9/11 revenge camp
established by the u.s. at Guantanamo, from where images of
orange-clad prisoners first spread across the world. At no point is
the concert attender or DVD viewer called on to view them like
this; it seems instead that the costuming is primarily a way both of
breaking the fourth wall of the work of 'behind the scenes', and
of making their activity so easily identifiable that they become
invisible.

Although technological spectacle was very much to the fore
in the 'Growing Up' tour, so was Gabriel's habitual undermining
of the stadium concept concert. The literalism of 'Downside
Up', sung while walking tethered upside down (accompanied by
his daughter Melanie Gabriel on backing vocals), was the first
moment of self-aware high absurdity; the song 'Growing Up'
featured the zorb ball, in which Gabriel rolled around the stage,
pausing to hop it up and down periodically. The ball signified the
way in which play is still possible in adulthood, and beyond that
obvious idea was a sort of cyborg embodiment where the individual is given heightened power from within the ever-moving
technological landscape; the bike riding of 'Solsbury Hill' while
dodging band members on the rotating stage worked as a
meta-commentary on the strangeness of what he was actually
doing, through the medium of the contemporary fashion for
urban cycling or the 'need' to stay fit. Over the years, 'Solsbury
Hill' in live settings had gone from being a joyously simple
statement of freedom to being a crowd-inspiring Big Tune, and
the bike dissipated the overblown state it had got into by then.
Spatially, geographically, the concern was with mobility within
and across contemporary spheres of activity, while acknowledging
the part played by labour in enabling digital and technological
freedoms.

The album was more serious, a claustrophobic tour through
states of mind and society familiar from the four *Peter Gabriel*

albums. Like the show, and like its predecessor in *ovo*, contemporary technology was highly present, in the audible use not only of multitracking, collaging and sampling but also of digitally generated sounds. This made *Up* a more networked version of the topographies expressed in *Big Blue Ball* and *ovo*. This world was one where proximity has become something excessive, where only heavy use of available soft- and hardware can restore equilibrium – a balance that is explicitly taken away in the closing track, 'The Drop'. The album's post-millennial feel, like a nostalgic echo of the Y2K bug that would never arrive, is signalled and developed in 'Darkness', the opening track.

In 'Darkness', Gabriel returns, as if a lost traveller, to his own self-inspection as mirrored through psychoanalysis. The track plays out broader cultural fears and announces the world of *Up* as one of the slow loss of familiar connections, and one that is fracturing into separate, often dangerous, perhaps fatal realities. Gabriel's voice is processed as he outlines his fears; then his voice clears, moving 'up' in the mix as well, as he masters them, only for him to whisper-walk us into 'the woods', where 'the deeper I go, the darker it gets', a lateral depth to the downward rootling of 'Digging in the Dirt'. These are archetypal woods, a darkness that is always near to us even as we raze trees and light up our mass human environments. These are not the woods bordering the sheep-filled fields of *Big Blue Ball*, but their other, a dark companion. 'Darkness' also introduces the punctuating effect of digitally produced sound, at its loudest here and in 'Signal to Noise' towards the end of the album. Through the track, a greater audibility of the digital (here in the form of loud, treated stabs of sound designed to shake the listener on the way into the wood walk) announces threat.

'Growing Up' continues in a more psychological lyrical vein, and counterbalances the house in the woods with the narrator's 'looking for a place to live', such that the process of ageing is one of dwelling, of self-locating. As in 'Darkness', the material world is accompanied by another (represented by Gabriel's ghost that likes to travel), with this spiritual drift creating structure through spectral mapping. As heard on *Us* almost a decade earlier, located-ness is always about negotiating the physical; here, this is through the drifting in and out of it, in proximity to another ('folded in your fleshy purse'). Underlying the track's jaunty tone of ranging discovery, matched in its music, there is still an undercurrent of electronic, programmed and keyboard sound that keeps up the sense of trouble lurking nearby. The same goes for the more utopian, 'upward' tracks of the album, 'Sky Blue' and 'More than This', with the measured, constant layers of electronics awaiting the eruption they finally receive in the cloudburst of 'Signal to Noise'. In 'More than This', the sense of a greater reality is accompanied by dread, in both lyrics and the long notes that precede the revelatory chorus. The 'more' that 'I' see in the song is not so much spiritual, but a sense of 'feeling so connected', along with the existence of a world that is constantly overflowing the mundane concerns that individuals are caught up in, or thrown into. Even as the 'I' of the song praises a self-aware connection 'right next to you', we still hear elongated, slowed sounds (I think from guitars) and skittering, a thrumming undertow of the possibility of both 'more' and 'this' being snatched away. 'Sky Blue' is simpler, launched by languorous keyboard, with other sounds joining gradually, and in fact begins with loss – 'lost my time, lost my place' – but as it goes on, it transforms into a journey where attaining the realm of 'more' becomes more audibly possible (this is achieved through the building presence of vocal group the Blind Boys of Alabama).

As is often the case, physical location acts as transposition of mental states – one example being the need to keep moving to retain stability. This gestures to a wider reality of 'connected' society, where being is increasingly constructed through process, rather than fixed identity. Such ideas are what pull *Up* into something bigger than a series of complaints from a position of privileged angst. 'The Barry Williams Show' and 'My Head Feels Like This' are over-literal in their approach to newly configured informatic society, so it is when Gabriel uses the capacity to abstract, and be musically and lyrically suggestive, that the album surfaces as an almost Ballardian take on contemporary society, a view on the abstraction and angst that is somehow fostered in capitalistic uses of communications acceleration.

The more direct stories on *Up* suggest a fearful narrator, but Gabriel is assessing the fearfulness that spreads through media representations of contemporary dangers, as well as as a result of the dangers in their own right. 'I Grieve', for example, is not just about a disaster that has appeared from nowhere, but is based on Gabriel's fear that something had happened to his daughters, who were present in New York on 11 September 2001, and the subsequent discovery that they were in fact safe, so the situation resolved.[20] In the song, then, the hour that passes is the trace of the disappearance of loss, replaced by the fear of a possible disaster, which then does happen. More than a personal tale, or a story from the media, 'I Grieve' is about how mediatized society processes the world as something immediate, flickering between complete knowledge and the shock of the event. There is a hopeful message in the song, conveyed by the closing musical section, a gentle, dancing rhythm, with the words dominated by variants of 'life carries on', but even here that is 'in the flies and rats / in the rot and the rust'. 'No Way Out' works on similar, parallel levels as a crowd of onlookers tries to stave off the death of someone fallen.

It is possible of course to try and read the actual person Peter Gabriel through the musings of *Up*, to see a man under threat, a world of difference closing in. It would be easy, but facile, to see the use of the process of abstracting as a denial of material oppression or exploitation in the world. A quick glance to the parallel musical worlds of *Big Blue Ball* and *ovo* should dismiss conjectures about privileged alienation, as the world in multiple and complex ways not only intrudes into Gabriel's thinking and emotion, but is recognized and mobilized in many ways as part of the overall mission of seeking locatedness through dislocations.

The album's closing couplet of songs, 'Signal to Noise' and 'The Drop', take two different aspects of contemporary life: communications and their use and abuse in the former and machine-based terrorism in the second. Both these tracks are about the states of fear that are being established through state and para-state organizations, controlling the thinking and actions of those who travel in the contemporary world. Those who travel means everyone, because the 'ghosts' that travel do so along the cables of the Internet as much as on forms of physical transit. 'Signal to Noise' begins in epic fashion, with strings, thick percussion and Gabriel's slightly leering declamation of an end to come. The signal is what will counter the noise ('Turn up the signal / Wipe out the noise'). Generally, noise is seen as something that hinders communication, meaning, truth, familiarity, even music, but here it is an active and maleficent presence, with the rising voice of Nusrat Fateh Ali Khan fighting the darkness of failing communication, the rising pitch and yaw of strings and mounting percussion, culminating in Gabriel's rallying call to 'receive and transmit'.

When the narrator speaks of 'the world turning to noise', this seems to indicate a sense of 'the world' that is different to that of Gabriel's predominantly liberal humanist view of the world as at least having the potential for unity. Perhaps by 2002, the sense of liberal consensus was coming somewhat under threat by 'global' events – but more relevantly, the mediatization of global communications is what creates the panic of noise in perception and reception. Signal is needed as clarity, a prospect not structured by fear. There is another way of seeing the noise, as the breaking free of limitation-based and supposedly consensual realities, but it is very interesting *how* Gabriel sees the increase in communication, and, by implication, more usage of what others think of as noise-making technologies: social media, more traditional media now re-mediated in Internet pulses instead of Hertzian waves. One solid example of this is the now common practice of filming oppressive and/or violent acts, which Gabriel pioneered through the Witness organization. Far from withdrawal, Gabriel is talking about the risky but necessary embrace of the technologized, globalized but not coherent world as the set of processes 'we' (everyone in the world) should dwell in, as opposed to being subject to them.

'The Drop' dissipates the percussive drive of 'Signal to Noise', its conflation of people throwing themselves from the World Trade Center and passengers on a weaponized plane clearly warning of the dystopian and asymmetrical reality that was becoming visible to people in the West in 2002. The warning, though, is about the need to reflect, analyse and dwell in the connected communicational world, and to not ignore events or treat them as merely reasons for fear. Again, as for J. G. Ballard, angst is the subject under discussion, rather than being the state or the definitive perspective of the narrator, whose cool and anomic take on what is going on is an expression of what subjectivity is like *after* being fearful, and where menace or dread are not just impressions but a set of knowing processes, mobilized as cultural weaponry.

The world that stretches out panoramically in the collaborative albums and *Up* is one of mood become global, of communication becoming more and less than a choice. Communication will simply happen; the question is not our attitude to it but what we do, or what it does to us. More than engagement, this period of Gabriel's work shows his meshing of models of globalization as experienced by the transitory presence of individual human lives in constant hybrid redefinition through cultural encounters. The backdrop, however, becomes bleaker, and what were internal states of anomie now play out on colossal scale, in many cases imposing identity as a means of control, exploitation or destruction. The foreground of Gabriel's collaborations, combined with his involvement in Witness, illustrate the potential for a parallel, 'other' process of globalizing, based on cooperative use of dis-location as a type of citizenship.

8 RETURNS

The outward-bound, inward-exploring positioning of the decade
leading to *Up* transformed as Gabriel took in a more global vista
and as the first decade of this century advanced. The work of
the beginning of the century concluded with the appearance of
Long Walk Home, Gabriel's album version of the soundtrack to
Rabbit-proof Fence (2002). Like *Passion*, this album uses a wealth
of instrumentation and musical modes to convey an atmosphere
driven by long tones, bass notes and rhythms. Musicians from
several continents, including singers from Australia's Indigenous
peoples, combine acoustic elements with electronic elements and
digital mixing and recording. The 'return' in this album was the
central story of the film, that of the Indigenous child characters
escaping enforced resettlement in an orphanage, most likely
as disciplining preparation prior to being forcibly adopted by a
white family in the widespread government-led process (from
the beginning of the twentieth century right up to the 1970s) of
diminishing, even eradicating, the peoples who had first dwelled
in Australia.

Tracking the 'rabbit-proof fence' northward, two of the three
children not only return home, but in so doing undermine the
whole process of enforced 'civilizing', and reassert the value of
learned experience about their environment. The music of the
album pursues the film's narrative of return through the thematic
reprise of two pieces of music, one of which would also appear

on *Up* as 'Sky Blue'. The latter part of the album features longer
tracks and gives retrospective structure to the whole, in keeping
with the outlook of *Rabbit-proof Fence*. This explicitly musical
mapping of recovery (and of self-reflective journeying) makes its
own return towards the end of the first decade of the new century. In between *Long Walk Home, Up*, the 'Growing Up' tours and
the new projects, Gabriel was busy elsewhere: there were vocal
contributions to others' work, appearances of individual songs in
soundtracks, and the new song 'Down to Earth' took its bow in
Wall-E (2008). There was also extensive involvement in developing
new music software and delivery systems, most notably in the
form of We7, launched by Gabriel and Steve Purdham in 2007
and ultimately bought by Tesco in 2012 and rebranded under the
Blinkbox name. In 2007 Gabriel became one of The Elders, a
self-appointed group of wise people with the capacity to intervene on a global level, that is, with access to, but outside, political
systems and identified political ties (unlike elected politicians).
This not-at-all-sinister-sounding group's mission was to act on a
largely humanitarian basis – another vehicle for Gabriel's liberal
humanist, pragmatic politics.[1]

But it would be 2010 before new work under his own name,
in extended form, would appear. The work from this decade can
be thought of in terms of returning. A new musical approach
– predominantly Western classical – was the bedrock, and with
this came the reinterpretation of others' songs in *Scratch My
Back* (2010), and reinterpretations by others of his work in *And
I'll Scratch Yours* (2013), bringing Gabriel back to where he began;
as he put it in an interview in 2010, 'songwriting was really the
passion that focused my attention on music in the beginning.'[2]
Gabriel observed that while the cover album was not in itself a
great idea (referring to the 'dreaded covers album'), he said that
'if I got a song-swap off the ground then it would mean that there
would be a dialogue and some relationship with the other writer.'[3]

At the same time, Gabriel was working up a new body of his own work in the shape of *New Blood* (2011), an extensive revisitation and reimagining of his career. Other returns included his involvement in the remastering and reissuing in 2008 of the canonical Genesis albums from his period as vocalist (1967–75), and the 25th anniversary enlarging and restructuring of *So* in 2012; this was also accompanied by a tour featuring the album played in full, on the 'Back to Front' tour (2012–14). Like the cover albums, Gabriel had also been uncertain about making such a statement about the past, but changed his mind after seeing Brian Wilson revisit The Beach Boys' pioneering 1966 album *Pet Sounds* in concert:

> I never really wanted to do the retro thing . . . but when I went to see Brian Wilson do *Pet Sounds*, I thought, actually, seeing the people who made one of your favourite records performing it is a special thing, and maybe I should look again at this.[4]

In 2016, the first four of his solo albums (and their German versions) came out on vinyl, followed by all the later albums. While those records made their material appearance, new tracks also appeared – 'I'm Amazing', about Muhammad Ali, and 'The Veil', made for Oliver Stone's film about u.s. security whistleblower Edward Snowden. Gabriel also went on a u.s. tour ('Rock Paper Scissors') with Sting.

The massive campaign of developing his own material is a complete phase in its own right in the developing story of how Gabriel situates himself in his own mind and in the minds and ears of others. It should not be seen as a rejection of his more overtly experimental work, or of his hitherto constant seeking out of hybrid music forms, or the contributions of new collaborators. Instead, it flowed on from the remixes done by others (notably

Trent Reznor, Röyksopp, The Polyphonic Spree) of tracks from *Up*. Revisiting was not a return to the safety of home but a way of seeing how home has changed. In other words, another dislocation was at work, even with what seems to be more familiar work. In reflecting on the decisions behind *New Blood* – but which apply to this whole phase of his work – Gabriel said that it was important to 'accept and acknowledge where you've come from and still be exploring things that are interesting and exciting', revealing different dimensions that were not previously brought out.[5] The return was a way of drilling into the walls of home, a more abstracted way of approaching the question of what identity is, of how psychological impulses, events and passing time play out across the words and notes of songs already complete but now revealed as unfinished, as potentials for change.

The idea of the covers album was that the two parts should occur at once, with Gabriel covering the songs of others while those same musicians covered his songs. Time constraints prevented this aspect of the project from reaching timely fruition, hence the separate appearance of the albums (since reunited as *Scratch My Back . . . And I'll Scratch Yours*, 2013). Gabriel's notion was that his choices of songs and choices made by others from among his songs would lead to a peculiar reconfiguration of the idea of collaboration, with shared material performed and recorded separately but as if together (this is in fact how Gabriel and Sting conceived their joint tour in 2016, with some tracks done as collaborations, some sung by the original singer, others by the other). As well as the collaborative aspect, each artist would bring their presence to the cover, having discussed ways of doing this beforehand. For Gabriel this presence would, he imagined, be based on combining 'references from what you're doing and references from what they already know of the song', such that the reflection on collaboration, on outwardness, extended to the prospective listener.[6] The twinned covers albums would represent an extension of the shared space of collaboration of *Big Blue Ball* or *ovo*. Not every musician accepted the deal, even if most did, so the albums do not mirror each other as much as was imagined at the outset. The songs do not pair up as such, but Gabriel released six batches of two songs, with the original writer of each song in turn doing a version of one his songs. Of these, the pairing with Elbow seems more of a connected unit, with their song 'Mirrorball' not too distant from a Tony Banks-led early Genesis song (Gabriel comments in the liner notes on the difficulty of the vocal, as the demands were similar to some of the early Genesis songs). The pairing with Lou Reed is more curious, with Gabriel smoothing out the ragged romanticism of 'Power of Your Heart', and Reed repaying the favour with a bristling and distorted 'Solsbury Hill'. The albums do form something of a pair when brought together, and they both advance the sense of personal locatedness of the artist in a significant way.

The idea of the cover version is one specific to the age of rock music – even as pop and rock 'n' roll took off in the 1950s, the idea of ownership of a popular song took one of two polar opposite forms: either it was a traditional form of commons, or it was the property of songwriter and publishing company. The idea changed once musicians got their hands on all aspects of the making of records (if not all the rights or the royalties) in the 1960s. In late 1950s France, Jacques Brel changed the rules within the *chanson* tradition, writing both music and lyrics and perform-ing the resulting songs. It is perhaps for this reason that one of the great sets of covers is of his work, by Scott Walker (*Sings Jacques Brel*, released in 1981 from recordings in 1967–9), asserting his own creativity not through the use of open access as such, but as a direct and royalty-paying act of worship. The development of the cover version or cover album is too large a discussion for here, but Walker's album raises the key points for a rock musician (or those in its splinter genres) engaging with the songs of others rather than their own: respect for the musician and music concerned, and re-presentation of your roots. Gabriel had shown this in his performances of soul songs on his early tours. David Bowie had done the same, very consciously addressing his sources with tunes mostly from 1960s London, on his *Pin Ups* (1973), at the same time as Bryan Ferry released his quasi-crooning covers album *These Foolish Things*. Much like being able to draw well, the ability to make good versions of 'standards' is a demonstration of prowess, even more so if you can stamp your musical identity on the songs as opposed to simply inserting your own vocals.

By 2010, the world was full of cover versions, cover albums, and tribute bands specializing in getting as close to the original sound of a band as possible (not least the reconstructions of Gabriel-era Genesis shows by The Musical Box or ReGenesis). Original bands tour as tributes to themselves, musicians remake albums, rework tunes. This is happening in every conceivable genre, as is the remix, the collision of two or more tracks, the collaging and deconstruction of works. As if this were not enough, swathes of talent shows cross media platforms to bring covers of 'great songs', and also of particular vocal styles, in the name of real musical talent. So, the appearance of the cover project by Gabriel might be unexpected from him, but it arrives into a world somewhat replete with ways of remaking a song.

Gabriel's answer, in addition to pushing the collaborative angle on *Scratch My Back*, was to introduce restrictions, the key to which, revealed in the liner notes, was the absence of guitar and drums. In fact, the arrangements, by John Metcalfe, were essentially orchestral – albeit not often using a complete orchestra at any one time. Once this was established as the default method, Gabriel and Metcalfe decided to push a further parameter into the remit, which was to recreate the effect of the work of composers such as Arvo Pärt, or the American minimalists. This decision brings the album closer to the way in which jazz musicians try their hand at 'standards', usually bringing a unifying, preselected aesthetic to bear, through the choice of a certain group of musicians, for example. Within rock and pop, bands have done the same sort of thing in choosing a unifying musical aesthetic (such as the arch cuteness of the band Nouvelle Vague, who specialize in café jazz versions of goth music, and often seek to make two genres collide).

In *Scratch My Back*, it is the orchestral arrangement that brings the tracks together, perhaps more so than Gabriel's voice. The tracks are brought towards him and he adds his distinctive vocal. The album is very much a whole, due to the combination of the two elements, but it is more privative than additive – it is very much a simplifying reduction ('I'm learning better when to be empty and when to be full,' Gabriel told the *New York Times*), arguably to concentrate on 'the song itself'.[7] It also creates a sparse, unitary piece, an echo perhaps of Philip Glass's two symphonic renderings of David Bowie's *Low* and *Heroes* albums (both 1977, with the Glass versions 1992 and 1996 respectively). This is far from unlikely, given that the opening song of *Scratch My Back* is a sparse, elegiac rendering of 'Heroes' set in the mode of East European minimalist music, removing the spark of the achieving hero in favour of a resistant but doomed figure. The most distinctive cover follows, that of Paul Simon's 'The Boy in the Bubble' from 1986's *Graceland*. This choice is interesting given that album's foregrounding of South African music (some might argue that this is more of a backgrounding), and here all reference to that is gone. The original's fast and jaunty delivery meant that it conveyed a strong component of hope, along with the prospect of radical change and what the 1990s would get used to calling 'collateral damage'. In short, it was a complicated but not entirely bleak exploration of human technological creativity. Gabriel's version is post-apocalyptic, the wistful strings, following the solo piano, and the steady pace of the vocal strongly suggesting that

the 'miraculous' advances of today have been reduced to making
the best of very little amid the threat of technological warfare
and further destruction of the remnants of culture. In short, this
was a song that had been transformed into something of very
strong relevance to the global situation of 2010, while almost
coming from a parallel Earth where the possible termination of
this one has been made material. As this chimed so strongly with
Gabriel's own aesthetic as heard on *Up* and elsewhere, this was
where the taking ownership of a song was at its strongest on the
album.

It is in tackling 'The Listening Wind' (Talking Heads, from
Remain in Light, 1980, also an album known for its attempt to
fuse non-Western rhythms and structures with rock songs) that
Gabriel touches directly on a global concern: terrorism and the
motivations behind it. In the song, a man named Mojique system-
atically bombs Americans who have taken over his village. Even
with its abstraction or modern mythological reading of a bomb-
er's motivations, the strange and stately original rendering of the
story created an effective, balanced setting for a meditation on
political violence, and the further honing of the track by Gabriel
adds a starkness to the choice made by its central character. In
these two tracks, Gabriel continues to invest in the world around
him, superficially worried by the absence of global unity. More
accurately, he is haunted by the prospect of people separating
from the world, and of their world therefore becoming small
and leading them to act on the threat of others. Once again, as
on *Up*, he comments on those fears and signals the possibility of
unity through the multitracked vocals, incidentally illustrating
the strength that can rally behind a cause, whatever our thoughts
on its mission delivery. In the lyrics of 'The Listening Wind',
the village is pitted against global commerce and power, and its
speculations are brought into more abrupt relevance by Gabriel's
careful reworking of the track.

The rest of the album comprises a mix of songs of then recent vintage with the older, more established classics mentioned here. The selection – of tunes by Bowie, Paul Simon, Elbow, Bon Iver, Talking Heads, Lou Reed, Arcade Fire, The Magnetic Fields, Randy Newman, Regina Spektor, Neil Young and Radiohead – was chosen by Gabriel in collaboration with David Bates and Anna and Melanie Gabriel. The choices were all very mainstream, and in most of the versions, initial dramatic twists and turns were replaced by the piano, the orchestra and steady vocals, with the result being an absenting of identity from the songs.

The taut, minimal arrangement and measured pacing leads to a strong focus on the voice. So, though we might not be able to say that the songs have the stamp of Gabriel's intervention, they certainly witness his presence. The use of the untreated, unchanging voice is a test of an exposed self – this is Gabriel's voice as interpretative device, as voice of the songs, rather than as controller of the material. In that sense, the album is a peculiar and subtle experiment in self-location: the voice of the self that is embodied becomes a tool in the service of other ends, even more so than in collaboration. At the same time as Gabriel's strongly clear vocals play out very much on top of the music in *Scratch My Back*, the gesture of the album is one of self-effacement. Yet again, even when he seems most present, close attention to the processes at play reveal dis-location.

The process of making *And I'll Scratch Yours* (released in 2013, three years after *Scratch My Back*) was diametrically opposed, as Gabriel's written voice, via lyrics and music, radiated out through the interpretations of others. Twelve different artists offered as many varied approaches, and yet there was a unity – the song structure and the rhythmical interests of the chosen songs cohered as a shared continuity across many of the tracks. Where the first volume of the covers project saw Gabriel introject the songs of others, here it is 'the other' who listens to him, in order for

Gabriel in turn to listen to them, and himself, through their work. Individually, artists seemingly selected and appropriated songs they felt matched their established aesthetic (the 'references from what you're doing' that Gabriel said he was looking for), and therefore these covers have to be understood as something else for those artists: that is, it is only one song in their repertoire, the Gabriel song. But here, as the set of twelve they were engineered for, they offer facets of Gabriel that we have encountered before, but with the modification that the intense detail of Gabriel's musical settings is largely removed in favour of that of the covering artist. Gabriel's song DNA takes new forms but remains recognizably the product of his genotype. The remixes of tracks from *Up* had taken a different process, a kind of retroviral approach, digging into the tunes to splice in new material or recombine the existing elements. Here, the songs take off from Gabriel, just as they do in the 'hands' of listeners everywhere (using 'references from what they already know', as he put it), and it is not incidental that the returns embodied in this project and those of *New Blood*, or the tours that came after, are very much oriented to what the listener would find interesting in how Gabriel relives, reshapes and re-presents his work.[8]

Where *Scratch My Back* thrived on self-imposed limitations, with Gabriel saying of them that he was 'better trying to get around something than building something', the second volume was fated to head in the other direction, as many of the artists made extensive use of digital sounds and instrumentation, multitracking and editing, while Gabriel's own covers eschewed his increasingly habitual and extensive use of those methods, machines and wares.[9] This means that, overall, *And I'll Scratch Yours* had a wider sound palette, but perhaps one that was less surprising, maybe even less thoughtful, despite the input of so many others. The exceptions to this – the tracks that presented an analysis of the track as part of their reading – crowd towards the end of the album: Leslie Feist joins with the band Timber

Timbre to reverse the narrator roles in 'Don't Give Up', and Brian Eno and Lou Reed provide the strongest reconfigurations, with 'Mother of Violence' and 'Solsbury Hill' respectively. The album ends with a dramatic yet unengaged acoustic guitar-based 'Biko' from Paul Simon. Like some of the other covers, and the cover version as genre or practice, this version pays no heed to the importance of textures, arrangements and structure. Eno makes no such mistake.

'Mother of Violence', from the second *Peter Gabriel*, originally co-written with Jill Gabriel (though listed on this album as by Peter Gabriel), was a misleadingly gentle song, with guitar, piano and Fripp's buzzing guitar hum underpinning lyrics about the fears induced by media, by ideologies we all consume. In that version, it was 'fear' that was the 'mother of violence', personified at the beginning of the song. Eno's rereading transforms the idea, such that we can imagine a more explicit and conscious creation of fear by a 'mother of violence'. The details of the activities are laid out with plosive emphasis in the verses, and the chorus is 'She's the mother of violence', with fear absented from the chorus rather than present in every line of it. Alone on this album, Eno's 'Mother of Violence' subscribes to Gabriel's millennial reading of the world, where the global atmosphere of menace is built up through media manipulation and asymmetric threat.

'Solsbury Hill' is the strangest reimagining – and if Gabriel's bicycle riding on the 'Growing Up' tour had deflated its easy acceptance as crowd-pleasing epic, then this goes further and darker. The darkness is filled with gleeful absurdity as Reed trundles through lyrics with a very vague semblance to the line and verse structure, and replaces all the sounds in any preceding version of it with dirty, almost rusty, crunchingly distorted guitar. Reed's seemingly brooding take on the dark landscape of old Albion revels in the absurdity of finding freedom on somewhere as quiet and banal as a hill, whatever its associations. Despite the presence of 'Biko' after it, in a mirroring of the structure of the many shows that Gabriel ended on that track, this 'Solsbury Hill' is where the project ends – the chewing up of the idea of a return, of an escape. From outside comes the confirmation that this was an escape that may once have had a role, a place for its place (the hill itself), which is now redundant. This does not stop it continuing onward, defamiliarized, at the end of so many iterations of Gabriel's voice on the first album, and so many reiterations of his written voice on the second. The ponderous chords slow the progress of the song (or appear to), such that the landscape loses its timeless 'quality' in favour of embedding in passing time, the passing of industrial society as well as of the agrarian, idealized past. Ultimately, Reed's version was a deep mourning, made real by its ridiculousness, emphasized in the various restatements of 'my heart's going boom boom boom' at the end, as a kind of puffing out of old breath, a vocal head shake. In that purposive demolition of the hill, Reed also evoked a different return, that of New York, which was as much at the core of Gabriel's transition from Genesis to solo performer as were the sentiments of 'Solsbury Hill'.[10]

The reimagining of his own oeuvre that was Gabriel's *New Blood* sat between the two parts of the cover project – in time, as it came out in 2011, but also in intent. This album saw Gabriel reinterpreting his own songs, using the orchestra as more of a sonic tool than as the unmovable and unchanging setting. The arrangements, by John Metcalfe and Gabriel, were more dramatic, more in resonance with the originals, even where they differed. For example, there is a significant use of percussion in opener 'Rhythm of the Heat', albeit significantly simplified from the original on *Peter Gabriel*. *New Blood* is essentially acoustic, although I presume some vocal treatment has occurred, with the piano slightly less to the fore than on *Scratch My Back* but still acting as a semi-regular counterpoint. On this album, the use of orchestra

feels less rigid, as if lessons were learned from the previous album.
In the liner notes, Gabriel outlines the how and why of the musical settings, writing that the use of orchestra for his own work had
been very limited, and until *Scratch My Back* had never constituted
the entirety of the musical setting of the songs. In restaging
these works from across his career, Gabriel also stipulated that
the music would not see endless massed strings overwhelming all
else (a tendency when rock bands collaborate with orchestras),
and more importantly, as far as I hear it, that the bass and rhythm
of the originals would be maintained, with 'a bass big enough
to drive the bottom end that I didn't often hear in conventional
classical mixes'.[11]

Without offering bass sounds or percussion the central role
they perform in Western rock in general, and in Gabriel's work
in particular, a certain dynamic of sound but also of musical narrative has to be transposed from rock. Very often on the album,
only small sections of the orchestra can be heard. There are also
numerous moments when Gabriel shares the singing, such as on
the fairly faithful reading of 'Downside Up' with Melanie Gabriel.
Faithful but not straightforward, in that Gabriel tries to approach
Paul Buchanan's voice on the original on *ovo*, when the latter had
been singing in a close approximation of Gabriel's voice. Gabriel
is not only covering himself, but covering a song performed first
by others. The covers project receives a further affirmation in this
almost uncanny move.

The orchestral sound effects some changes to the originals,
and the maintenance of rhythm has not precluded something of
a re-Westernization of Gabriel's music, as many of the complex
musical (and cultural) layerings noted in previous chapters are
stripped away in favour of a skeletal recentring of the tunes. This
is Gabriel's music as European product, perhaps, more than a
return to Albion. The use of orchestra also needs to be distin-
guished from progressive rock's high-art aspirations. Very few

New Blood being performed live in London, March 2011.

progressive rock bands sought to replicate the actual form and sound of classical music, and when they did, it was firmly in the context of jazz and the idea of fusing musical forms. The idea of a stripped-back or mutated 'classical' palette was rare in English progressive rock, if more present in the work of groups in Rock in Opposition such as Univers Zéro or Magma.

The second disc on the expanded CD version of *New Blood* consists of the instrumental versions of virtually the full set of songs on the first one (other than 'Blood of Eden', which closes the second set), and it is even clearer that the orchestra has not been used as ornament or pretext for overextension of tracks. What is striking about the music is how it retains the structures and the movement of the originals while sounding altered. The difference between the 'original' and *New Blood* versions is not additive, but transformative. This mode of return is about reconfiguring, recombining. It is more like the methodology of a remix rather than a cover – the tracks are not reimagined as if new, but as if renewed. This album is a stronger expression of Gabriel's perpetual reflection on his own development, this time applied not to his thoughts, views of the world, or relations with people and place, but applied to the way he has previously done those things. The word 'deconstruction' is overused in the sense of 'seeing how things are made', but here it works – these versions look into the songs in order to transform the way in which the sounds and words communicate meaning.

New Blood makes this aural reflection tangible and vivid once the idea of orchestrating the songs is understood as material in the project of expressing self and its location. The mere sound of the orchestra summons soundtracks – of course, far from the sounds Gabriel has used for his own film work, but functioning as an indicator, even director, of emotional reaction. The selectivity of instrumentation prevents the album being a reduction of the world into 'the classical'. There are a myriad classical and/ or acoustic takes on careers, but this one gains its purpose from the long-standing explorations and changes in direction that to a large extent define Gabriel's oeuvre. The overall effect is almost that *New Blood* is a soundtrack of the best of Gabriel, one where Gabriel comes in to reinterpret his own role (as illustrated even more strangely in 'Downside Up'). Where the music does intervene more expressively, let's say, than on the existing songs, it is to heighten aspects already there, often the more dissonant elements. In short, where *Scratch My Back* created a unified and stately sound field for the different songs to be ingested, here each track, and the album as a whole, seeks momentum through change. I find that this effect is bolstered by the decision to stick to the original divisions of verses, choruses and instrumental parts very closely, and then let the sounds and the new vocal do the work. The transformations on offer are based on interpretation and on dwelling in the songs, rather than wishing they had been totally different in the first place.

The selection of songs is not a greatest hits, but could easily be seen as a 'best of', in that the vast majority of tracks included have featured on many of Gabriel's tours and live releases, and therefore have been chosen not according to a sense of popularity, but on the basis of their dynamic presence. 'The Rhythm of the Heat' and 'San Jacinto' keep their slowly mounting sense of exploration; many of the songs have interesting rethinkings, while varying more in the detail than in the overall effect. 'In Your Eyes' is a great example of this, its staccato strings a way of achieving exactly the same effect as the original, but with totally different means. Most interesting are the darker songs, such as 'Intruder' and 'Darkness'. Both of these feature Gabriel taking up the positions of characters via the way he sings. The sombre and sneaky tones of the 'Intruder' on *Peter Gabriel* give way to a more gleeful, assertive nastiness, with the anger that drives the intruder character ramped up in the choruses. In 'Darkness', Gabriel sings the verses in a lurchingly monstrous tone, as if possessed by the Oliver Reed of a 1970s horror film, perhaps. The section where the narrator goes into the woods, conquering the demons represented in the verses, is taut, much more embodied, where the track on *Up* had a meandering feel, dissipating tension in the several changes it underwent. This new version is pleasingly overblown, its transitions rendered more meaningful, able to catch the intent of the noise stabs of the original. Where 'Darkness' layers music, lyrics and vocals into a consistent if fracturing whole, 'Digging in the Dirt' contrasts a relatively tranquil musical setting, the dominant strings tuneful if quizzical, with an angrier, more difficult narrator even than the one seen and heard in previous versions. In fact, Gabriel's adoption of a very threatening delivery here is an extension of how the song when presented live had tightened its focus on that part, having initially (on the 'Secret World' tour in particular) looked at the self-exploration angle and treated the 'shut your mouth' section as a momentary disturbance as opposed to the defining instance of the 'digging', as it is on *New Blood*.

The album closes on 'Solsbury Hill', much less predictably than it might seem, as Gabriel writes that he was persuaded to include it, but only if it could be separated from the rest of the album. The divider was to have been silence, but this was replaced by a few minutes of field recording from the eponymous hill (in the vinyl form of the album release, these two tracks are kept apart on a 7-inch single). Initially resistant, Gabriel was keen to distance himself from the song, even as he compromised, so did not do the recording himself: 'that song grew out of sitting on Solsbury Hill meditating, so what I'll do is ask [Real World sound engineer Richard Chappell] to go up Solsbury Hill and grab some ambience.'[12] In the end, Gabriel's insistence on downplaying the track has lent it huge sonic significance. A straight reading of 'The Nest that Sailed the Sky' gives way to that field recording, entitled 'A Quiet Moment' – birds, wind, distant traffic and the sounds of walking through grass provide a literal but not socially unaware pastoral. This is the countryside as actually experienced, 'tainted' by sounds the ear can censor but among which the microphone does not discern. Here, then, is the real place (we are told, and have to presume), uncoded, and presented only as heard. This does not mean that the track can be thought of as an objective moment in a world of objects expressing themselves: the recorders (person and machine) were there, the idea of recording as a way of capturing the real was in play, and then a section was selected (even if the 4:48 of the track is 'the whole'), and today's listeners can understand a field recording as akin to a photograph, an index of an actual reality, in which someone or something was somewhere. The track is almost a gift; it is a place rendered different through the abstraction of itself onto the album in 'A Quiet Moment'. The title adds to its definition: on the album it is a break, an actualization as well as a representation of relaxation.

This tranquillity is the precise mood of the lyrics of 'Solsbury Hill', as discussed earlier, and in closing *New Blood* it remains calm, purposely laid back. Gabriel's singing is as close to a crooning style as he gets (but still reassuringly far), downplaying the acquired anthemic quality of the song. Even Lou Reed's mangling of the song had played up the rousing side of its message of freedom in his caustic repetitions of 'boom boom boom'. As the song closes, Gabriel repeats that he is coming home, and the album,

Solsbury Hill, the location that titles Gabriel's first solo hit single, to which he returns in the lyrics of later releases.

which was a commentary on his oeuvre, receives its own meta-level commentary – a further *dis-located* song, finding, locating and moving all at once, a point from which directions extend.

The sequencing of the album does not contain a particular message, but it does head towards the more utopian, out-ward-looking Gabriel of the more recent releases – 'The Nest that Sailed the Sky' from the utopian, forward-looking part of *ovo*, 'The Blood of Eden' by itself as vocal track at the end of the instrumental disc, and in between these there is the doubled 'Solsbury Hill' as another path out of the worldly and into aware-ness of a wider world. *New Blood* protracts Gabriel into different dimensions of locatedness, dwelling inside his work, but poised outside it simultaneously.

REFERENCES

PREFACE: GENETICS

1 In Len Brown, 'Black Steel in the Hour of Chaos', *New Musical Express*, 3 June 1989, www.rocksbackpages.com.

1 ALBION

1 Daryl Easlea, *Without Frontiers: The Life and Music of Peter Gabriel* (London, 2013), p. 30.

2 This is a well-rehearsed argument, one that informs Dominic Sandbrook's epic history *Never Had It So Good: A History of Britain from Suez to The Beatles* (London, 2005).

3 David Kynaston, *Modernity Britain, 1957–1962* (London, 2015), pp. 633–46.

4 Rob Young, *Electric Eden: Unearthing Britain's Visionary Music* (London, 2010).

5 Bob Carruthers, *Genesis: The Gabriel Era* (China, 2004), p. 9.

6 Easlea, *Without Frontiers*, p. 45.

7 Carruthers, *Genesis*, p. 22.

8 Ibid.

9 Gabriel, liner notes, *Genesis 1970–1975* (Virgin, CDBOX14, 2008).

10 Gabriel, liner notes to the 'Extras' CD, in *Genesis 1970–1975*.

11 Banks, liner notes to 'Extras' CD, in *Genesis 1970–1975*.

12 Raymond Williams, *The Country and the City* (St Albans, 1973), p. 83.

13 Michael Watts, 'Reading from the Book of Genesis', *Melody Maker*, 23 January 1971, available at www.genesismuseum.com.

14 Gabriel quoted in Paul Morley, *Ask: The Chatter of Pop* (London, 1986), p. 91.

15 Max Bell, 'Genesis: Gabriel's Cosmic Juice', *New Musical Express*, 15 March 1975, available at www.rocksbackpages.com.

16 Williams, *The Country and the City*, p. 29.

17 Georgina Boyes, *The Imagined Village: Culture, Ideology and the English Folk Revival* (Leeds, 2010).

18 See Colin Harper, *Dazzling Stranger: Bert Jansch and the British Folk and Blues Revival* (London, 2006), pp. 38–57.

19 Trish Winter and Simon Keegan-Phipps, *Performing Englishness: Identity and Politics in a Contemporary Folk Resurgence* (Manchester, 2013), p. 114. See also Boyes, *The Imagined Village*, pp. 12 and 63.

20 Carruthers, *Genesis*, p. 39.

21 William Morris, *'News from Nowhere' and Selected Writings and Designs* [1890] (Harmondsworth, 1984), pp. 183–301.

22 Michael Moorcock, *The Final Programme* (New York, 1968).

23 John Grindrod, *Concretopia: A Journey around the Rebuilding of Postwar Britain* (Brecon, 2013).

24 Jerry Gilbert, 'Genesis Doing the Foxtrot', *Sounds*, 9 September 1972, available at www.rocksbackpages.com.

25 Carruthers, *Genesis*, p. 59.

26 Sarah Hill advances these terms for the two dominant registers in Gabriel's voice, in 'From the New Jerusalem to the Secret World: Peter Gabriel and the Shifting Self', in *Peter Gabriel: From Genesis to Growing Up*, ed. Michael Drewett, Sarah Hill and Kimi Kärki (Farnham, 2010), pp. 15–29.

27 Easlea, *Without Frontiers*, p. 104.

28 William Blake, *Jerusalem: The Emanation of the Giant Albion* [1804–20], plate 27, in *The Illuminated Books* (London, 2001), pp. 298–397.

29 Ibid., plate 79.

30 Ibid., plates 99–100.

31 Winter and Keegan-Phipps, *Performing Englishness*, pp. 105–13.

32 Paul Hegarty and Martin Halliwell, *Beyond and Before: Progressive Rock since the 1960s* (New York, 2011), pp. 140–43.

33 Bridging these two in 1970s Worthing was the sub-Wimpy restaurant The Golden Egg.

34 Ron Ross, 'Genesis: The Future of Rock Theatre', *Phonograph*, February 1975, available at www.rocksbackpages.com.

2 NEW YORK, NEW YORK

1 William Blake, *America, a Prophecy* [1793], in Blake, *The Complete Illuminated Books*, pp. 154–72 (plate 8).

2 Gabriel, in Bob Carruthers, *Genesis: The Gabriel Era* (China, 2004), p. 100.

3 Gabriel in Chris Welch, 'The New Face of Gabriel', *Melody Maker*, 26 October 1974, available at www.rocksbackpages.com.

REFERENCES

4 Gabriel, in Carruthers, *Genesis*, p. 99.

5 Gabriel, in Ron Ross, 'Genesis: The Future of Rock Theatre', *Phonograph*, February 1975, available at www.rocksbackpages.com.

6 Banks in *Genesis 1970–1975* (Virgin, 2008) interview DVD; Mike Rutherford, *The Living Years* (London, 2014), p. 144.

7 Gabriel in *Genesis 1970–1975* (Virgin, 2008), interview DVD.

8 See Paul Hegarty and Martin Halliwell, *Beyond and Before: Progressive Rock since the 1960s* (New York, 2011), pp. 86–8.

9 Rutherford, *The Living Years*, p. 147.

10 Hackett in *Genesis 1970–1975* interview DVD.

11 Hackett and Collins in *Genesis 1970–1975* interview DVD.

12 Rutherford, *The Living Years*, pp. 150 and 157; Banks in *Genesis 1970–1975* interview DVD.

13 See Daryl Easlea, *Without Frontiers: The Life and Music of Peter Gabriel* (London, 2013), pp. 142–4 and 128 respectively.

14 Ross, 'Genesis: The Future'.

15 Kevin Holm-Hudson, *Genesis and 'The Lamb Lies Down on Broadway'* (London, 2008), p. 64.

16 Ibid., p. 68.

17 Ross, 'Genesis: The Future'.

18 Gabriel in Max Bell, 'Gabriel's Cosmic Juice', *New Musical Express*, 15 March 1975, available at www.rocksbackpages.com.

19 Holm-Hudson, *Genesis and 'The Lamb'*, pp. 64 and *passim*.

20 For an exploration of the realities of Puerto Rican identities in New York, see Virginia E. Sánchez Korrol, *From Colonia to Community: The History of Puerto Ricans in New York City* (Berkeley, CA, 1983).

21 See Rutherford, *The Living Years*, p. 147.

22 Joshua Shannon, *The Disappearance of Objects: New York Art and the Rise of the Postmodern City* (New Haven, CT, and London, 2009), p. 4.

23 For a table of the crime rates in New York from 1960 to 2015, see www. disastercenter.com, accessed 5 May 2017. The rate was consistently around 2,000 every year from 1972 to 1983, and between 1987 and 1994, and really only dropped off dramatically after 1998.

24 See Rem Koolhaas, *Delirious New York: A Retroactive Manifesto for Manhattan* [1978] (New York, 1994).

25 See Holm-Hudson, *Genesis and 'The Lamb'*, p. 130, for a full account of the American show, pop and rock tunes that are referred to on the album.

26 Gabriel in Max Bell, 'Gabriel's Cosmic Juice'.

27 Collins in *Genesis 1970–1975* interview DVD.

28 Barbara Charone, 'Interview: Peter Gabriel Talks', in *New Musical Express*, 13 October 1973, available at www.rocksbackpages.com.

29 Gabriel, in Chris Welch, 'The New Face of Gabriel', *Melody Maker*, 26 October 1974, available at www.rocksbackpages.com.

30 Gabriel, in Chris Welch, 'In the Beginning There Was . . . Genesis', *Melody Maker*, 24 April 1971, available at www.rocksbackpages.com.

31 Charone, 'Interview: Peter Gabriel Talks'.

32 Gabriel did play 'The Knife' on at least one occasion. For full details of these early tours, see www.halleyandpeter.nl, accessed 1 December 2016.

3 PETER GABRIEL, PETER GABRIEL, PETER GABRIEL, PETER GABRIEL

1 Penny Valentine, 'The Lamb Brought Down in Paris', *Melody Maker*, 23 December 1978, available at www.rocksbackpages.com.

2 Peter Gabriel and Stewart Kranz in interview with Mikal Gilmore, *Rolling Stone*, 22 February 1979, available at www.rollingstone.com.

3 In Barbara Charone, 'Say Goodbye to the Bubble Creature', *Circus*, 17 March 1977, available at www.rocksbackpages.com.

4 Gabriel in interview with Andy Green: 'Peter Gabriel: Story that Bruce Springsteen was Inspiration for "Solsbury Hill" is "Hogwash"', 10 October 2011, www.rollingstone.com, accessed 15 May 2017.

5 In an interview from 1982, Gabriel would refer to 'a little hole in the ground in the Lake District – it's like a three-foot waterfall, in a marshy pit' as one of his favourite English locations, highlighting a sense of nature as arbitrary and our interaction with it as somewhat absurd (Richard Cook, 'Rhythm of the Pete', *New Musical Express*, 2 October 1982, available at www.rocksbackpages.com).

6 In Caroline Coon, 'Peter Gabriel', *Sounds*, 24 June 1978, available at www.rocksbackpages.com.

7 In Valentine, 'The Lamb'.

8 Ibid.

9 In Coon, 'Peter Gabriel'.

10 Gabriel, at www.petergabriel.com, accessed 17 May 2017.

11 Fripp, in interview with Jean-Gilles Blum in *Best*, January 1979, available at www.elephant-talk.com.

12 In Valentine, 'The Lamb'.

13 In Sutcliffe, 'Mr Clean: Peter Gabriel', *Sounds*, 14 June 1980, available at www.rocksbackpages.com.

14 See www.petergabriel.com, accessed 21 May 2017.

15 Dave Marsh, 'Peter Gabriel, *Peter Gabriel*', *Rolling Stone*, 18 September 1980, available at www.rollingstone.com.

16 The German versions of *Peter Gabriel* (1980) and *Peter Gabriel* (1982), entitled *Ein deutsches Album* and *Deutsches Album* respectively, are a curious aside to Gabriel's dis-locations. The version of the third *Peter Gabriel* is very straight-forward, little more than a re-singing of the lyrics in German (although 'Biko' is extended), whereas *Deutsches Album* is more like a remix. The recording quality is even higher, almost all of the tracks are tweaked instrumentally as well as lyrically, and the whole offers a more electronic mood than that on the original fourth *Peter Gabriel*.

17 In Sutcliffe, 'Mr Clean'.

18 Paul Virilio, *Speed and Politics: An Essay on Dromology* [1977], trans. Mark Polizzoti (New York, 1986).

19 In Sutcliffe, 'Mr Clean'.

20 Ibid.

21 Ibid.

22 Michael Drewett outlines the specific and different songs used on different versions. The single used the ANC anthem, now that of South Africa, 'Nkosi Sikelel' iAfrica' (Drewett, 'The Eyes of the World are Watching Now: The Political Effectiveness of "Biko" by Peter Gabriel', in *Peter Gabriel: From Genesis to Growing Up*, ed. Michael Drewett, Sarah Hill and Kimi Kärki (Farnham, 2010), pp. 99–111 (p. 103).

23 Ibid.

24 Gabriel's concern with creeping state control, as well as a more or less inevitable social sanctioning of wrongness or otherness, was visualized on his tours in 1978 and 1980, where the bands wore a uniform garb. On the first of these tours, it was approximate: white top (complete white outfit for Gabriel) with orange high-visibility bibs, appropriate for state-run safety organizations. In the second, the whole group wore matching black jump-suits. In 1980 many musicians, across the spectrum, presented themselves in this way, quite possibly illustrating concerns with the authoritarianism of the then new Thatcher administration in Britain, which came to power in May 1979.

25 Cook, 'Rhythm of the Pete'.

26 Ibid.

27 Edward W. Said, *Orientalism: Western Conceptions of the Orient* [1978] (London, 1991).

28 Ibid., pp. 326–8.

29 Charles Forsdick, *Victor Segalen and the Aesthetics of Diversity: Journeys between Cultures* (Oxford, 2000), p. 210.
30 William Burroughs and Allen Ginsberg, *The Yage Letters* [1963] (San Francisco, CA, 1986).

4 REAL WORLD

1 See Michael Drewett, 'The Eyes of the World are Watching Now: The Political Effectiveness of "Biko" by Peter Gabriel', in *Peter Gabriel: From Genesis to Growing Up*, ed. Michael Drewett, Sarah Hill and Kimi Kärki (Farnham, 2010), pp. 106–7. Phil Sutcliffe, 'Organised Chaos: Peter Gabriel', *Q*, May 1989, available at www.rocksbackpages.com.
2 Sutcliffe, 'Organised Chaos'.
3 WOMAD poster, 1982.
4 Famous Western musicians had staged events to raise money and awareness before this, perhaps most notable being the case of George Harrison's 'Concert for Bangladesh', starting out as a set of two concerts in Madison Square Garden, New York City, on 1 August 1971, then going on to take shape as a film and triple album of the same name.
5 See www.petergabriel.com, accessed November 2016.
6 In Len Brown, 'An Alien in the Real World', *New Musical Express*, 10 June 1989, available at www.rocksbackpages.com.
7 Philip V. Bohlman, *World Music: A Very Short Introduction* (Oxford and New York, 2002).
8 Ibid., p. i.
9 In interview with Terry Wogan, on the *Wogan* TV programme, 1987. Available at www.youtube.com, accessed 24 May 2017.
10 Martin Stokes, 'Globalization and the Politics of World Music', in *The Cultural Study of Music: A Critical Introduction*, ed. Martin Clayton, Trevor Herbert and Richard Middleton (New York, 2012), pp. 107–16 (p. 107).
11 Steven Feld, 'From Schizophonia to Schismogenesis: On the Discourses and Commodification Practices of "World Music" and "World Beat"', in Charles Keil and Steven Feld, *Music Grooves* (Chicago, IL, 1994), pp. 257–89 (p. 266).
12 Ibid.
13 Franck Buioni, *Peter Gabriel: Real World* (Rosières-en-Haye, 2009), p. 283.
14 On Papa Wemba's rock influences, see Anicet Etou Nianga, *Papa Wemba: La voix de la musique congolaise moderne* (Paris, 2014), pp. 30–31.
15 Timothy D. Taylor, '"Nothin' But the Same Old Story": Old Hegemonies, New Musics', in *Peter Gabriel*, ed. Drewett, Hill and Kärki, pp. 131–9 (p. 131),

and originally part of Taylor, *Global Pop: World Music, World Markets* (London and New York, 1997).

16 Free jazz musicians were exploring African themes, rhythms, modes as part of a new cross-cultural fusion that was more excessive than the 'fusion' genre, and was deeply politicized, particularly by musicians active in Chicago and New York.

17 Laurent Aubert, *La Musique de l'autre: les nouveaux défis de l'ethnomusicologie* (Chêne-Bourg and Geneva, 2011), p. 99, my translation.

18 See Lloyd Bradley, *Sounds Like London: 100 Years of Black Music in the Capital* (London, 2013), pp. 19–59.

19 Aubert, *La Musique de l'autre*, p. 1.

20 In Sutcliffe, 'Organised Chaos'.

21 Steven Feld, 'Notes on "World Beat"', in Kiel and Feld, *Music Grooves*, pp. 238–46. Timothy D. Taylor makes a similar point about Peter Gabriel, in 'Nothin' But the Same Old Story', but Dave Laing points out that this type of critique seems never to have heard of 'solo artists' who employ many players, including their friends, or well-known musicians, orchestras or 'world musicians', without forfeiting 'ownership' through the common act of putting their name on the album as the sole artist. See Laing, 'Hand-made, Hi-tech, Worldwide: Peter Gabriel and World Music', in *Peter Gabriel*, ed. Drewett, Hill and Kärki, pp. 141–56 (p. 144).

22 Taylor, 'Nothin' But the Same Old Story', p. 131.

23 Feld, 'From Schizophonia to Schismogenesis', p. 265.

24 David Thompson and Ian Christie, eds, *Scorsese on Scorsese* (London, 1989), p. 139.

25 Ibid.

26 Gabriel, in Brown, 'An Alien in the Real World'.

27 Ibid.

28 In Johnny Black, 'Peter Gabriel: World Party', *Q*, November 1991, available at www.rocksbackpages.com.

29 Len Brown, 'Black Steel in the Hour of Chaos', *New Musical Express*, 3 June 1989, available at www.rocksbackpages.com.

5 *SO* AND THE GLOBAL NETWORK

1 Francis Fukuyama, *The End of History and the Last Man* (London, 1992).

2 Andrew Goodwin, 'Fatal Distractions: MTV Meets Postmodern Theory', in *Sound and Vision: The Music Video Reader*, ed. Simon Frith, Andrew Goodwin and Lawrence Grossberg (London and New York, 1993), pp. 45–66 (pp. 49–52

in particular). This chapter is a condensation of Goodwin, *Dancing in the Distraction Factory:* MTV, *Music Television and Popular Culture* (Minneapolis, MN, 1992).

3 As noted by David Fricke, senior editor of *Rolling Stone*, in *Peter Gabriel: So (Classic Albums)* DVD (Eagle Rock, 2012).

4 Gabriel in Phil Bell, 'Peter Gabriel: Tales of the Gold Monkey', *Sounds*, 1 October 1983, available at www.rocksbackpages.com.

5 Progressive rock theorist Holm-Hudson notes that 'Sledgehammer' saw Gabriel bringing his early inspirations to the fore. In 'How Peter Gabriel Got His Mozo Working', in *Peter Gabriel: From Genesis to Growing Up*, ed. Michael Drewett, Sarah Hill and Kimi Kärki (Farnham, 2010), pp. 43–55 (pp. 43–5 and pp. 51–2 in particular).

6 As commented on by John Richardson in 'Plasticine Music: Surrealism in Peter Gabriel's "Sledgehammer"' and by Brenda Schmahmann in 'Staging Masculinities: Visual Imagery in Peter Gabriel's "Sledgehammer" Video'. Both in *Peter Gabriel:*, ed. Drewett, Hill and Kärki, pp. 195–210 and pp. 57–69 respectively.

7 Schmahmann, 'Staging Masculinites', p. 64.

8 Animator David Sproxton makes this precise point, describing using Gabriel 'as an animated model' (*So*, 25th Anniversary Box, Real World, PGBOX2, 2012, liner notes; hereafter *So* 25).

9 Richardson, 'Surrealism in Peter Gabriel's "Sledgehammer"', p. 197.

10 Georges Bataille, *Eroticism* [1957], trans. Mary Dalwood (London, 1987). p. 31.

11 *So* 25, liner notes.

12 Ibid. Easlea presents this set of images and ideas well, addressing the context of the time (Daryl Easlea, *Without Frontiers: The Life and Music of Peter Gabriel*, London, 2013, pp. 250–51).

13 *So* 25 liner notes.

14 Carol Vernallis, *Experiencing Music Video* (New York and Chichester, 2004), p. 254.

15 According to Vernallis, writing on the video's connections to Sexton and to the lyrics, 'in "Mercy St.", when the viewer makes up a story about the life of a young Sexton, the video loses its radical edge – in this instance, the video's interest in blanking out, absence and negation' (ibid., p. 269).

16 Ibid., p. 257.

17 *So* 25, liner notes.

18 *Peter Gabriel: So (Classic Albums)* DVD (Eagle Rock, 2012).

19 Franck Buioni, *Peter Gabriel: Real World* (Rosières-en-Haye, 2009), pp. 249–51.

6 ALL OF US

1 All references to Real World's 'mission' are from https://realworldrecords.
2 Peter Gabriel, *Passion: Sources* (Real World, RWCD2, 1989), liner notes.
3 Peter Gabriel, at www.petergabriel.com, accessed 30 May 2017.
4 Ibid.
5 Ibid.
6 On the technical elements of the recording process of *Us* and the use of a massive variety of non-Western instruments, see Richard Buskin, 'Peter Gabriel: Digging in the Dirt', *Sound on Sound*, November 1992, pp. 78–82.
7 Serge Lacasse, 'The Introspectionist: The Phonographic Staging of Voice in Peter Gabriel's "Blood of Eden" and "Digging in the Dirt"', in *Peter Gabriel: From Genesis to Growing Up*, ed. Michael Drewett, Sarah Hill and Kimi Kärki (Farnham, 2010), pp. 211–23.
8 Julia Kristeva, *Strangers to Ourselves*, trans. Leon S. Roudiez (Hemel Hempstead, 1991), pp. 57–61.
9 Gabriel, in Robert Sandall, 'Peter Gabriel: Gawp Factor Ten', *Q Magazine*, July 1993, available at www.rocksbackpages.com.
10 Ibid.
11 Ibid.
12 Ibid.
13 William Gibson, *The Peripheral* (London, 2015).
14 See https://witness.org.

7 THE LOCAL IN THE GLOBAL, THE GLOBAL IN THE LOCAL

1 Homi Bhabha, *The Location of Culture* (London and New York, 1994), p. 1.
2 Jocelyne Guilbault used Bhabha as a core reference in her important article of 1997 reflecting on how to theorize world music. In that context, Bhabha's use of hybridity stood out as a way of moving beyond notions of authenticity or misrepresentation. Guilbault , 'Interpreting World Music: A Challenge in Theory and Practice', *Popular Music*, XVI/1 (1997), pp. 31–44.
3 In Christopher R. Weingarten, 'Peter Gabriel Reflects on 25 Years of Real World', www.rollingstone.com, 17 October 2014.
4 See Simon Frith, 'The Discourse of World Music', in *Western Music and Its Others: Difference, Representation, and Appropriation in Music*, ed. Georgina Born and David Hesmondhalgh (Berkeley and Los Angeles, CA, 2000), pp. 305–22 (p. 307).
5 Ibid., p. 312.

6 The question of sampling musicians from 'other cultures' is explored in David Hesmondhalgh, 'International Times: Fusions, Exoticisms and Antiracism in Electronic Dance Music', in *Western Music and Its Others*, ed. Born and Hesmondhalgh, pp. 280–304. Readers might note the change in the use of the term EDM since the turn of the century.

7 Georgina Born and David Hesmondhalgh, 'Introduction: On Difference, Representation, and Appropriation in Music', in *Western Music and its Others*, ed. Born and Hesmondhalgh, pp. 1–58 (p. 42).

8 Ibid., p. 19.

9 Real World Records, '10 Years of Real World Records', available at www. youtube.com, accessed 31 May 2017.

10 Steven Feld, 'The Poetics and Politics of Pygmy Pop', in *Western Music and Its Others*, ed. Born and Hesmondhalgh, pp. 254–79 (p. 263).

11 See http://bigblueball.realworldrecords.com, accessed 10 December 2016.

12 Ibid.

13 Kofi Agawu, *Representing African Music: Postcolonial Notes, Queries, Positions* (New York and Abingdon, 2003), pp. xx and pp. 168–9.

14 This is what makes transnational noise music so interesting, because it uses shared non-language to undermine the idea of shared language that differentiates music from noise.

15 Others do contribute lyrics to the album, and stick closely to the blueprint of 'the big question'. Iarla Ó Lionáird contributes a verse to 'Altus Silva' on the inevitability of death and the need to embrace life.

16 Sagan muses on the meaning of this perspective in his *Pale Blue Dot: A Vision of the Human Future in Space* (New York, 1994).

17 Gabriel, on the 'mission' of the show and OVO, www.petergabriel.com, accessed 10 December 2016.

18 For a melancholic and critical reading of the Dome and its effect on the surrounding areas, see Iain Sinclair, *Sorry Meniscus: Excursions to the Millennium Dome* (London, 1999).

19 See for example Saskia Sassen, *The Global City: New York, London, Tokyo* (Princeton, NJ, 1991), and various writings at www.saskiasassen.com.

20 See Daryl Easlea, *Without Frontiers: The Life and Music of Peter Gabriel* (London, 2013), p. 327.

8 RETURNS

1 See www.theelders.org. The idea was devised by Richard Branson and Gabriel. The latter is part of the 'advisory council'.

2 In interview with Jude Rogers, *The Guardian*, 2 June 2010, www.theguardian.com.

3 See www.petergabriel.com.

4 In interview with Stuart Maconie: 'Peter Gabriel – Interview', BBC6, 26 September 2014, available at www.bbc.com.

5 Gabriel on 'Blood Donors' feature, *New Blood – Live in London*, DVD (Real World/Eagle, 2011).

6 See www.petergabriel.com.

7 In Jon Pareles, 'Peter Gabriel Says "I'll Sing Yours, You Sing Mine"', *New York Times*, 1 March 2010, www.newyorktimes.com.

8 See www.petergabriel.com.

9 In Pareles, 'Peter Gabriel Says'.

10 Lou Reed performed an even more torn-up version, with many 'boom boom boom's, at a New York show in 2010, early in the covers project: available as 'Lou Reed – Solsbury Hill – LIVE NYC 3 May 2000' at www.youtube.com, accessed 5 November 2016.

11 Gabriel, *New Blood*, 2 CD version (Real World, PGCDX13, 2011), liner notes.

12 In interview with John Doran, www.thequietus.com, 19 September 2011.

BIBLIOGRAPHY

BOOKS ON PETER GABRIEL

Bowman, Durrell, *Experiencing Peter Gabriel: A Listener's Companion* (Lanham, MD, 2016)

Bright, Spencer, *Peter Gabriel: An Authorized Biography*, 2nd edn (London, 1999)

Buioni, Franck, *Peter Gabriel: Real World* (Rosières-en-Haye, 2009)

Carruthers, Bob, *Genesis: The Gabriel Era* (China, 2004)

Drewett, Michael, Sarah Hill and Kimi Kärki, eds, *Peter Gabriel: From Genesis to Growing Up* (Farnham, 2010)

Easlea, Daryl, *Without Frontiers: The Life and Music of Peter Gabriel* (London, 2013)

Holm-Hudson, Kevin, *Genesis and 'The Lamb Lies Down on Broadway'* (London, 2008)

GENERAL

Agawu, Kofi, *Representing African Music: Postcolonial Notes, Queries, Positions* (New York and Abingdon, 2003)

Aubert, Laurent, *La Musique de l'autre: les nouveaux défis de l'ethnomusicologie* (Chêne-Bourg and Geneva, 2011)

Bataille, Georges, *Eroticism* [1957], trans. Mary Dalwood (London, 1987)

Bell, Max, 'Genesis: Gabriel's Cosmic Juice', *New Musical Express*, 15 March 1975, available at www.rocksbackpages.com

Bell, Phil, 'Peter Gabriel: Tales of the Gold Monkey', *Sounds*, 1 October 1983, available at www.rocksbackpages.com

Bhabha, Homi K., *The Location of Culture* (London and New York, 1994)

Black, Johnny, 'Peter Gabriel: World Party', *Q Magazine*, November 1991, available at www.rocksbackpages.com

Blake, William, *America, a Prophecy* [1793], in Blake, *The Complete Illuminated Books* (London, 2001), pp. 154–72

—, *Jerusalem: The Emanation of the Giant Albion* [1804–20], in Blake, *The Complete Illuminated Books* (London, 2001), pp. 298–397

Bohlman, Philip V., *World Music: A Very Short Introduction* (Oxford and New York, 2002)

Born, Georgina, and David Hesmondhalgh, eds, *Western Music and Its Others: Difference, Representation, and Appropriation in Music* (Berkeley and Los Angeles, CA, 2000)

Boyes, Georgina, *The Imagined Village: Culture, Ideology and the English Folk Revival* (Leeds, 2010)

Bradley, Lloyd, *Sounds Like London: 100 Years of Black Music in the Capital* (London, 2013)

Brown, Len, 'An Alien in the Real World', NME, 10 June 1989, available at www.rocksbackpages.com

—, 'Black Steel in The Hour of Chaos', *New Musical Express*, 3 June 1989, available at www.rocksbackpages.com

Burroughs, William, and Allen Ginsberg, *The Yage Letters* [1963] (San Francisco, CA, 1986)

Buskin, Richard, 'Peter Gabriel: Digging in the Dirt', *Sound on Sound*, November 1992, pp. 78–82

Canclini, Néstor García, *Hybrid Cultures: Strategies for Entering and Leaving Modernity*, trans. Christopher L. Chiappari and Silvia L. López (Minneapolis, MN, 1995)

Charone, Barbara, 'Interview: Peter Gabriel Talks', *New Music Express*, 13 October 1973, available at www.rocksbackpages.com

—, 'Say Goodbye to the Bubble Creature', *Circus*, 17 March 1977, available at www.rocksbackpages.com

Clayton, Martin, Trevor Herbert and Richard Middleton, eds, *The Cultural Study of Music: A Critical Introduction* (New York and London, 2012)

Cook, Richard, 'Rhythm of the Pete', *New Musical Express*, 2 October 1982, available at www.rocksbackpages.com

Coon, Caroline, 'Peter Gabriel', *Sounds*, 24 June 1978, available at www.rocksbackpages.com

Doran, John, 'Interview with Peter Gabriel', *The Quietus*, 19 September 2011

Feld, Steven, 'From Schizophonia to Schismogenesis: On the Discourses and Commodification Practices of "World Music" and "World Beat"', in Keil and Feld, *Music Grooves*, pp. 257–89

—, 'The Poetics and Politics of Pygmy Pop', in *Western Music and Its Others*, ed. Born and Hesmondhalgh, pp. 254–79

Forsdick, Charles, *Victor Segalen and the Aesthetics of Diversity: Journeys between Cultures* (Oxford, 2000)

Frith, Simon, 'The Discourse of World Music', in *Western Music and Its Others*, ed. Born and Hesmondhalgh, pp. 305–22

Fukuyama, Francis, *The End of History and the Last Man* (London, 1992)

Gibson, William, *The Peripheral* (London, 2015)

Gilbert, Jerry, 'Genesis Doing the Foxtrot', *Sounds*, 9 September 1972, available at www.rocksbackpages.com

Goodwin, Andrew, *Dancing in the Distraction Factory: Music Television and Popular Culture* (London, 1992)

—, 'Fatal Distractions: MTV Meets Postmodern Theory', in *Sound and Vision: The Music Video Reader*, ed. Simon Frith, Andrew Goodwin and Lawrence Grossberg (London and New York, 1993)

Green, Andy, 'Peter Gabriel: Story that Bruce Springsteen was Inspiration for "Solsbury Hill" is Hogwash', *Rolling Stone* 10 Ovctober 2011, www.rolling-stone.com.

Grindrod, John, *Concretopia: A Journey around the Rebuilding of Postwar Britain* (Brecon, 2013)

Guilbault, Jocelyne, 'Interpreting World Music: A Challenge in Theory and Practice', *Popular Musics* XVI / I (1997), pp. 31–44

Harper, Colin, *Dazzling Stranger: Bert Jansch and the British Folk and Blues Revival* (London, 2006)

Hegarty, Paul, and Martin Halliwell, *Beyond and Before: Progressive Rock since the 1960s* (New York, 2011)

Holm-Hudson, Kevin, 'How Peter Gabriel Got His Mozo Working', in *Peter Gabriel*, ed. Drewett, Hill and Kärki, pp. 43–55

Jarry, Alfred, *Ubu* (Paris, 1978)

Keil, Charles, and Steven Feld, *Music Grooves* (Chicago, IL, 1994)

Koolhaas, Rem, *Delirious New York: A Retroactive Manifesto for Manhattan* [1978] (New York, 1994)

Kristeva, Julia, *Strangers to Ourselves* [1988], trans. Leon S. Roudiez (Hemel Hempstead, 1991)

Kynaston, David, *Modernity Britain, 1957–62* (London, 2015)

Laing, Dave, '"Hand-made, Hi-tech, Worldwide": Peter Gabriel and World Music', in *Peter Gabriel*, ed. Drewett, Hill and Kärki, pp. 141–56

Marsh, Dave, 'Peter Gabriel, *Peter Gabriel*', *Rolling Stone*, 18 September 1980, available at www.rocksbackpages.com

Moorcock, Michael, *The Final Programme* (New York, 1968)

Morley, Paul, *Ask: The Chatter of Pop* (London, 1986)

Morris, William, *News from Nowhere and Selected Writings and Designs* (Harmondsworth, 1984)

Mundy, John, *Popular Music on Screen: From Hollywood Musical to Music Video* (Manchester and New York, 1999)

Nianga, Anicet Etou, *Papa Wemba: La voix de la musique congolaise moderne* (Paris, 2014)

Pareles, Jon, 'Peter Gabriel Says "I'll Sing Yours, You Sing Mine"', *New York Times*, 1 March 2010, www.newyorktimes.com

Richardson, John, 'Plasticine Music: Surrealism in Peter Gabriel's "Sledgehammer"', in *Peter Gabriel*, ed. Drewett, Hill and Kärki, pp. 195–210

Rogers, Jude, 'Interview with Peter Gabriel', *The Guardian*, 2 June 2010, www.theguardian.com

Ross, Ron, 'Genesis: The Future of Rock Theatre', *Phonograph*, February 1975, available at www.rocksbackpages.com

Rutherford, Mike, *The Living Years* (London, 2014)

Sagan, Carl, *Pale Blue Dot: A Vision of the Human Future in Space* (New York, 1994)

Said, Edward W., *Orientalism: Western Conceptions of the Orient* (London, 1991)

Sandall, Robert, 'Peter Gabriel: Gawp Factor Ten', *Q Magazine*, July 1993, available at www.rocksbackpages.com

Sandbrook, Dominic, *Never Had It So Good: A History of Britain from Suez to the Beatles* (London, 2005)

Sassen, Saskia, *The Global City: New York, London, Tokyo* (Princeton, NJ, 1991)

Sinclair, Iain, *Sorry Meniscus: Excursions to the Millennium Dome* (London, 1999)

Stokes, Martin, 'Globalization and the Politics of World Music', in *The Cultural Study of Music*, ed. Clayton, Herbert and Middleton, pp. 107–16

Sutcliffe, Phil, 'Mr Clean: Peter Gabriel', *Sounds*, 14 June 1980, available at www.rocksbackpages.com

—, 'Organised Chaos: Peter Gabriel', *Q magazine*, May 1989, available at www.rocksbackpages.com

Taylor, Timothy D., *Global Pop: World Music, World Markets* (London and New York, 1997)

—, '"Nothin' But the Same Old Story": Old Hegemonies, New Musics', in *Peter Gabriel*, ed. Drewett, Hill and Kärki, pp. 131–9

Valentine, Penny, 'The Lamb Brought Down in Paris', *Melody Maker*, 23 December 1978, available at www.rocksbackpages.com

Vernallis, Carol, *Experiencing Music Video: Aesthetics and Cultural Context* (New York and Chichester, 2004)

—, *Unruly Media: YouTube, Music Video and the New Digital Cinema* (Oxford, 2013)

Virilio, Paul, *Speed and Politics: An Essay on Dromology* [1977], trans. Mark Polizzoti (New York, 1986)

Watts, Michael, 'Reading from the Book of Genesis', *Melody Maker*, 23 January 1971, available at www.genesismuseum.com

Weingarten, Christopher R., 'Peter Gabriel Reflects on 25 Years of Real World', www.rollingstone.com, 17 October 2014

Welch, Chris, 'In the Beginning There Was . . . Genesis', *Melody Maker*, 24 April 1971, available at www.rocksbackpages.com

—, *Genesis: A Complete Guide to Their Music* (London, 2006)

—, 'The New Face of Gabriel', *Melody Maker*, 26 October 1974, available at www.rocksbackpages.com

Williams, Raymond, *The Country and the City* (St Albans, 1973)

Winter, Trish, and Simon Keegan-Phipps, *Performing Englishness: Identity and Politics in a Contemporary Folk Resurgence* (Manchester, 2013)

Young, Rob, *Electric Eden: Unearthing Britain's Visionary Music* (London, 2010)

WEBSITES

The Elders: www.theelders.org/about
Peter Gabriel: www.petergabriel.com
Genesis Archive: www.thegenesisarchive.co.uk
Genesis Museum: www.genesismuseum.com
Halley and Peter's Genesis List: www.halleyandpeter.nl
Real World Records: www.realworldrecords.com
Rock's Backpages: www.rocksbackpages.com
Witness: www.witness.org
WOMAD: www.womad.co.uk

DISCOGRAPHY

PETER GABRIEL

Peter Gabriel (Charisma / Virgin, PGCD1, 1977)

Peter Gabriel (Charisma / Virgin, PGCD2, 1978)

Peter Gabriel (Charisma / Virgin, PGCD3, 1980)

Peter Gabriel (Charisma / Virgin, PGCD4, 1982)

Ein Deutsches Album (Charisma, CDS4019, 1980)

Deutsches Album (Charisma, 6302 221, 1982)

Plays Live (Charisma / Virgin, PGDL1, 1983)

Birdy (Charisma / Virgin, CASCD1167, 1985)

So (Charisma / Virgin, PG5, 1986)

Passion: Music for 'The Last Temptation of Christ' (Real World, RWCD1, 1989)

Us (Real World / Virgin, PGCD7, 1992)

OVO (Real World, PGCD9, 2000)

Up (Virgin / Real World, PGCD11, 2002)

Long Walk Home: Music from the Rabbit-proof Fence (Virgin, 4603 8 12238 2 6, 2002)

Scratch My Back (Virgin / Real World, PGCD12, 2010)

New Blood, 2 CD version (Real World, PGCDX13, 2011)

So, 25th Anniversary Box (Real World, PGBOX2, 2012)

And I'll Scratch Yours (Real World, PGCD14, 2013)

Scratch My Back . . . And I'll Scratch Yours (Real World, PGCD15, 2013)

PETER GABRIEL IN GENESIS

From Genesis to Revelation (Decca, SKL4990, 1969)

Trespass (Charisma, CAS1020, 1970)

Nursery Cryme (Charisma, CAS1052, 1971)

Foxtrot (Charisma, CAS1058, 1972)

Selling England by the Pound (Charisma, CAS1074, 1973)

The Lamb Lies Down on Broadway (Charisma, CGS101, 1974)
Genesis: Archive 1967–75 (Virgin, CDBOX6, 1998)
Genesis 1970–1975 (Virgin, CDBOX14, 2008)

OTHER

Passion: Sources (Real World, RWCD2, 1989)
Big Blue Ball (Real World, USLPRW150, 2008)

DVD AND OTHER MEDIA

CV (Virgin, 1987)
POV (Virgin, 1991)
Xplora1 (Real World / MacPlay 1993)
Secret World Live (Geffen, 1994)
Growing Up Live (Real World / WEA 2003)
Play: The Videos (Warner, 2004)
New Blood – Live in London (Real World / Eagle, 2011)
Live in Athens 1987 (Real World / Eagle, 2013)

ACKNOWLEDGEMENTS

For all their input, direct, indirect, musical, cultural or in other modes, I would like to thank Graham Allen, Patrick Crowley, Dan Guiney, Gary Genosko, Greg Hainge, Martin Halliwell, Michael Hoar, Jim Horgan, Eleni Ikoniadou, Kevin Kennedy, Vicky Langan, Melanie Marshall, Dave Murphy, Irene Murphy, Rory O'Brien, Daragh O'Connell, Brian O'Shaughnessy, Mick O'Shea, Romain Perrot, Eldritch Priest, Laura Rascaroli, Alex Rose, Declan Synnott, Albert Twomey and Scott Wilson.

For asking me, and for being a superlative editor, John Scanlan at Reaktion Books. For their sterling work in securing and granting permissions for lyrics and images, Rob Bozas and Joanna Crow.

For her keen-eyed, punctilious and solicitous reading and suggesting, as well as her many most excellent qualities, I dedicate this slender tome to Sarah Hayden, with all my love. Our life together is amazing, because you are.

PERMISSIONS

All lyrics by Peter Gabriel. Published by Real World Music Ltd/Sony ATV.

PHOTO ACKNOWLEDGEMENTS

The author and the publishers wish to express their thanks to the below sources of illustrative material and/or permission to reproduce it.

Author's Collection: pp. 17, 39, 55, 66, 73, 104, 144, 150, 174, 186, 217; Courtesy of Peter Gabriel Ltd: pp. 84, 85 top (Design Hipgnosis), 85 bottom (Design Malcolm Poynter), 167; Getty Images: pp. 46 (Waring Abbott), 68 (Evening Standard); Courtesy of Real World Records: pp. 213, 191.

INDEX